# More Equal Than Others

# More Equal Than Others

## Women and Men in Dual-Career Marriages

ROSANNA HERTZ



UNIVERSITY OF CALIFORNIA PRESS
Berkeley Los Angeles London

7/93

University of California Press
Berkeley and Los Angeles, California

University of California Press, Ltd.
London, England



Printed in the United States of America

1 2 3 4 5 6 7 8 9

*Library of Congress Cataloging-in-Publication Data*

Hertz, Rosanna.
More equal than others.

Bibliography: p.
Includes index.
1. Married people—Employment—United States.
I. Title.
HQ536.H47 1986 306.8′7 86–4325
ISBN 0–520–05804–6 (alk. paper)

Bookstores

*To Syd, Jerry, and Bob*

# Contents

# List of Tables

# Preface

My objective is to ask a big question in a small way. What will it take for men and women to be truly equal? Philosophers and social critics have answered this question in many complex ways, but most agree that men and women must have equal positions in central social and economic pursuits. More to the point, men and women must be economic equals if they are to be equal in other spheres of social life.

I have studied a small but growing segment of American society in which men and women are economic equals: dual-career married couples in the corporate world. In this book I examine men's and women's paths to their careers—how they got there and why—and assess what relative economic equality has meant for crucial aspects of these couples' shared and individual social lives. The question that inevitably arises from such an exploration is whether success in the work world has fundamentally changed the nature of marriage and family.

Through an analysis of their experiences, I will suggest that dual-career couples are "more equal than others" in two senses. First, their relative economic equality has made possible important shifts in their roles as husbands and wives. They relate to each other and to their relationship as partners with equivalent goals, aspirations, and pressures. The boundaries between "breadwinner" and "homemaker" are difficult to see when neither spouse can lay claim to higher status or greater influence based on who is working outside the home or who is making more money. Unlike two-paycheck marriages, in which the husband may have a career and the wife a job (or temporary employment), the dual-career couple holds greater potential for equality in marital roles. Second, "more equal than others" also refers to the ways in which equality for some couples may be contingent on the availability of other people, often married couples, for whom equality is not common. In drawing attention to how dual-career couples achieve labor market success and develop marital equality, it will also be essential to show how structures of occupational and family stratification aid in the process.

Dual-career couples are by no means the vanguard of the American population in consciously pursuing gender equality. Indeed, they are one of the results of a changing economy: the startling expansion of white-collar employment and the growth of career opportunities for female college graduates have combined to make two careers in one family a more likely option. The composition of the pool of potential mates for well-educated, occupationally mobile men and women has altered over the past two decades; when a career-oriented individual encounters a potential mate today, it is increasingly likely that the "candidate" will also have a career.

Although only a few of the men and women I interviewed for this book considered themselves "liberated," most are grappling with questions of gender equality and marital equity in response to the pressures of their work. Equally demanding careers, similar incomes, and concerns about finding a balance between work and family have forced these couples to act differently than their more traditional parents and one-career family peers. These two-career couples negotiate household responsibilities and develop innovative solutions to managing finances. They talk about symmetry and equality in the context of her career, his career, and their marriage. They cannot, as often happens in noncareer settings, devalue her career as supplemental or "targeted," without tarring his career with the same brush.

These men and women are participating in an important process of social change. That they do so *behaviorally* more than *attitudinally* argues for an often overlooked perspective on societal change: if behaviors are changed, attitudes congruent with the change will often follow. In this instance men and women who have benefited from the labor market shifts and the achievements of the women's liberation movement are becoming advocates of gender equality even though they were not initially proponents of this cause.

Becoming an advocate, however, is not quite the same as being one. The change process in which dual-career couples participate also requires that they cope with an extraordinarily powerful and robust system of societal values. As these men and women seek roles and relationships that will enable them to combine work and marriage, they run up against a conventional vision of success, which tempers their perception of what is possible. Success in this context means independence, self-sufficiency, and finding individual solutions to individual problems.

This definition of success is woven into the fabric of the American economy and, most important, into the very concept of a corporate career. Those who successfully pursue such careers adroitly combine personal drive and ambition with a commitment to organizational goals. Having a career in the corporate world means one must demonstrate uniquely individual qualities, while sacrificing excessive individualism in order to be a "team player." The economic rewards for playing the game—

as an individual and as part of the corporate team—are considerable.

Meshing two careers in one family stretches the conventional definition of success and may pose an alternative definition. The couples in this study have struggled to adhere to the conventional definition by using the economic rewards from their careers to buy independence and self-sufficiency and by developing individual solutions to problems such as housekeeping, childcare, and recreation. To compensate for two equal sets of demands on their time and physical energy, they hire somebody else to clean the house. Because they cannot be home to supervise their children, they hire someone else to do so.

In their efforts to cope with career, family, and household, they look to themselves, to the marketplace, and ultimately to their checkbooks for solutions. In only a few instances do they look to their employers, to other couples in similar situations, or to society for help. Making solutions part of the employment contract or becoming involved in communal efforts remains for most couples an unconventional and unlikely approach. "Because we make so much money," they say, "we should take care of ourselves."

Thus, for some gender equality may be achievable without fundamentally challenging the hegemonic notion of success. But, as I hope to show in this book, the process of change may still continue—led, paradoxically, by those whose personal drive for success stretches the limits of conventional definitions.

Besides wanting to explore the big question of male and female equality, I also felt compelled to study gender equality by my undergraduate students, many of whom are planning corporate careers. Currently, social work and teaching are out as career goals, and business careers and making money are in—Lee Iaccoca and Mary Cunningham have replaced Abbie Hoffman and Betty Friedan as inspirations. Students preparing for careers in business make it a point to know about the career paths and salaries of investment bankers, securities brokers, and partners in accounting firms. Yet for all their research and networking, they know very little about how they will meet the simultaneous demands of corporate careers and family life. Goaded by newspaper and magazine articles that detail the lives of men and women who "have it all," most students simply assume they can accommodate both work and family. The realities of juggling both these responsibilities escape even the best career strategist in the classroom.

Throughout the writing of this study, my dissertation committee (Janet Abu-Lughod, Howard Becker, Christopher Jencks, Janet Lever, and Allan Schnaiberg) offered support and encouragement, and I thank them for their patience and their comments on earlier drafts. The members of this committee had the wisdom to tell me to write a book, not a dissertation. Once I stopped worrying about what Marx, Weber, and Durkheim would say, I was ready to write the story of these couples in my own words. Several of my committee members have dual-career marriages; their personal experiences were of great help and insight. Allan Schnaiberg chaired the dissertation committee and guided my career as a graduate student at Northwestern University. I especially thank him for knowing when to challenge and push me and for knowing when to go easier.

The manuscript also benefited from the suggestions and criticisms of the following people: Walter Allen, Asa Baber, Arlene Daniels, William Gamson, Harriet Gross, Barbara Heyns, Jonathan Imber, Joseph Pleck, Lillian Rubin, R. Stephen Warner, Martin Whyte, and two reviewers for the University of California Press, Naomi Gerstel and Jacqueline Wiseman. Several of these people I have never met personally, and I particularly appreciate the time they took from their busy research and teaching schedules to respond to my request for comments and criticism. I would also like to thank my editor at the University of California Press, Naomi Schneider, for her support and enthusiasm for the project.

Joy Charlton, Chip Wood, and Vivian Walker shared the anxieties and elations of graduate school and first jobs with me, and I still rely on their advice and support. My dance classes and MCI's phone service provided me with much-needed outlets during the process of research and writing. A special thanks to Nancy Weiss Klein for the many nights she spent typing the dissertation and to the Wellesley College Faculty Awards Committee for providing the resources necessary to complete revisions on the manuscript.

I am especially indebted to Bob Thomas, who read every word of every version—and there were many. He helped me find the important ideas buried beneath sometimes half-baked thoughts. On later drafts, as my "theory consultant," he helped me to move beyond simply writing a "recipe book" for dual-career couples to confront the broader implications of these couples' lives. Equally important was his courage in moving to Boston so we would not have to continue commuting between cities. This move enabled us to meld two careers and a personal life. His belief in me, even when I stopped believing in myself, made a difference.

# 1

# THE NEW "MODERN COUPLE"?

THE DUAL-CAREER COUPLE has been hailed in the 1980s as the new ideal middle-class marital relationship. The popular press has highlighted this phenomenon, filling lifestyle or social issues sections with tales of such couples: She's a doctor and he's a lawyer, or he's a diplomat and she's a corporate consultant. They went to graduate school together, and after completing school, both went on to pursue their chosen careers. Each morning they awake, jog together, eat breakfast, and are off to their respective jobs. She flies off on Monday for a three-day business trip, and he leaves on Wednesday for a two-day business trip. Candlelight dinners, cultural events, and shared sports activities fill weekends. The same zeal and energy couples bring to their work, they also bring to their relationships. The message: the dual-career couple is glamorous.

There are also couples who work in different cities. Every other weekend, Cindy Brown, a chemist, bundles her six-month-old daughter into her car and drives one hundred miles for a conjugal visit. Her husband, Seymour Katz, a financial analyst, lives in downstate Illinois. He drives to Chicago with the couple's twelve-year-old daughter on alternate weekends. They have been married for fourteen years, and they have lived apart for six of them. And they are happy. So begins another exciting tale of the dual-career couple. The message: the dual-career couple is making it.

Stories of "America's New Elite," as *Time* magazine dubbed them, have captured the imagination and interest of the American population.[1] For years we've read such sagas, which are perhaps rivaled only by stories of the rich and famous. Earlier generations of young girls grew up on Cinderella and Snow White, dreaming of princes to carry them off so they too could live happily ever after. Young girls today dream a different plot. There is still the prince, but happily-ever-after now includes a career. The dreams of young men are not so easily characterized. For earlier generations, a man's success was envisioned in occupational and financial terms; boys dreamed of being rich, strong, and independent. Wives, for many, were beautiful, faithful, and supportive, important symbols of success, as were bright, cheerful children and a comfortable home. The dreams of young men today (willingly or unwillingly) often include a wife who also works, as well as a vision of building family, house, and future together.

There are seemingly no barriers to fulfilling this new

1. "America's New Elite" (*Time,* August 21, 1978). Other newspapers and magazines that have published articles in recent years about dual-career couples include *Business Week:* "The Upward Mobility Two Incomes Can Buy" (20 February 1978), "America's New Immobile Society" (27 July 1981); *Chicago Tribune:* "Jobs Keep Couples Cities Apart" (20 July 1980), "Love and Work" (8 March 1981), "Stress in Two-Career Families Puts Pressure on Employers, Too" (26 July 1981), "Couples' Dual Goals Pose Problems of Priorities" (12 October 1982); *New York Times:* "Finding the Right Career-Family Mix" (20 July 1980), "Many Young Women Now Say They'd Pick Family Over Career" (28 December 1980), "What's New with Dual-Career Couples" (6 March 1983); *New York Times Magazine:* "The Perils of a Two-Income Family" (27 September 1981), "Careers and the Lure of Motherhood" (21 November 1982); *Time:* "Marriage of the Minds" (6 March 1978), "The Perils of Dual Careers" (13 May 1985).

dream. Many young women believe not only that sex discrimination in the workplace is dead but also that the new 1980s man is looking for a wife who has an exciting, rewarding career just like his. The media offer an endless supply of stories about the successful female corporate executive and the happy dual-career couple. She knows how to dress, how to act in the board room, how to compete, and also how to be a team player with her colleagues. Not only is she accomplished in her chosen field, but she is also the perfect wife and mother. In her home dinner is served on time every night, the house is clean, her children receive "quality time," and she and her husband are mutually supportive of their respective careers. He remains aggressive in pursuit of career success, but his aggressiveness is now tempered by a "soft" side. He is an active participant in the broad range of family chores: he takes his turn at cooking, doing the laundry, cleaning the house, caring for the children, shopping, transporting the children and their friends, and participating in the P.T.A. and neighborhood groups. He takes parenting seriously—from prenatal care to birthing, nocturnal feedings, and beyond. In short, the traditional job of the wife becomes a shared career.

In this vision of shared careers and responsibilities, there are few, if any, conflicts and even fewer obstacles to happiness. It seems eminently feasible from these accounts that both a husband and wife should be able to devote themselves to their respective careers, find self-expression in their work, and also pursue a stable, intimate, and enriching family life. Therefore, young men and women not only assume that they can have it all—spouse, children, and career—but they also are encouraged to want it all. A full, well-integrated life is easy to come by, and it can be had at no personal cost.

## DUAL CAREERS: A CONTINGENT PHENOMENON

There is no question that the dual-career couple exists. It is not simply a media creation designed to sell newspapers, launch new women's magazines, or placate the women's movement. Yet the origins, the working, and the potential consequences of this new development remain largely unexplored; the ideals of sexual equality in the workplace and the family have an allure far beyond what is actually the case. To separate myth from reality and to provide an accurate understanding of the phenomenon of the dual-career couple, we must first consider its special nature.

The attention paid to those situations in which career and family are successfully combined overshadows the fact that there are simply not many dual-career couples. Moreover, the vast majority of instances in which wives work do not result in equality in the home or reflect lessening inequality in the workplace. Married women who work are often expected to do double duty as wage earners and domestic laborers (homemakers). Their employment is viewed as secondary, even when their income is not supplementary or targeted for a specific purpose (such as purchasing a household appliance, a new home, or a vacation). The money they bring in does not count for as much as their husbands' salaries. Many more married women work because the ravages of inflation (especially in the 1970s) and debt have made two incomes necessary to support a family.

The dual-career couple is overshadowed statistically by the fastest growing category of family in the United States: the female-headed household. According to 1980 census figures, 12.4 percent of families were headed by a single parent, whereas 10.6 percent were single-parent households in 1970; 10.2 percent of all families were headed by a female in 1980, as compared to 8.7 percent in 1970.[2] In contrast to single, female heads of households, married women with careers are glorified as "supermoms" or "superwomen"—women who have the ability to successfully integrate family life and work. Such honorific titles are not bestowed on noncareer working mothers. At best these women elicit sympathy for their lot; at worst they are blamed for creating the circumstances they must endure.

A major distinction must be made between "careers" and "jobs." Most women do not have careers; they have jobs. Careers involve employment in which some realistic expectation of upward occupational and financial mobility is expected and available. Careers most commonly begin within the salaried ranks of an organization (although they need not always do so) and provide a clear path for advancement from lower to higher levels of responsibility, authority, and reward (Wilensky, 1960). In contrast, jobs offer limited opportunities for advancement, responsibility, and authority, are paid by the hour, and promise little significant increase in financial reward for achievement or for longevity of employment. Despite the rapid increase in women's (especially married women's) participation in the labor force over the last twenty years, women still find, accept, or are relegated to jobs, not careers. The oft-cited statistics on women's overrepresentation in dead-end, low-paying work have been well documented (Oppenheimer, 1976). Women generally receive lower pay, work shorter hours (often part-time), and have less protection in employment than do men. Since far more women are likely to hold jobs than to have careers, the focus on

2. Alternately, the percentage of the population that is married has declined from 70.9 percent in 1970 to 60.9 percent in 1980. (Data from U.S. Bureau of the Census, 1980.)

married women with careers hardly reflects a typical circumstance.

Finally, the dual-career couple is a *contingent* phenomenon. This description is a major theoretical argument of this study and as such deserves a brief explanation here. Dual-career marriage assumes that the right combination of resources makes the integration of personal and professional lives easy. What is lacking in this facile analysis is an appreciation of the privileged status of those who have careers to begin with. One-half of a dual-career couple—the woman—who was interviewed for this study said it best:

> Not everyone can afford to live the way we do. You really need a six-figure income. I feel that the popular magazines like *Redbook* do women and marriages a disservice. Some of the articles sound like everybody can have a dual-career marriage. A lot of people read these articles and use the dual-career couple as the ideal marriage, but most marriages will by definition fall short of this ideal because of the money aspect. What I mean is, my secretary gets paid about the same amount of money as my housekeeper. Can my secretary afford to have the type of dual-career family we have—a full-time housekeeper who also cares for the children? The answer is no.

Not only do this woman's observations emphasize an important precondition for the dual-career family—a high income—but they also challenge another representation of these families: their self-sufficiency. In fact, the couple's capacity to sustain two careers (and to acquire them in the first place) often depends on the availability of someone else to perform, for a wage, the duties necessary to maintain the household. The dual-career couple can prosper professionally in part because there are other couples or individuals who do not.

## WORK AND FAMILY: THE SOCIOLOGICAL CONTEXT

My remarks about the special and contingent character of the dual-career couple are not intended to deny the reality of its existence as an emergent family form. Rather, they are intended to help assign the dual-career couple its appropriate context, namely, within a system of stratification in which inequalities in access to employment and to rewards for work create differential life opportunities for both individuals and families. Four arguments are basic to understanding this context.

First, work and family are closely connected. The organization of work reflects the dominant functions of the economic system, creates the hierarchy of opportunities and rewards available, and determines both the financial position and the social status of family members. Work organizes family life inasmuch as it determines the amount of resources available for consumption, and it thereby affects the range of social and economic opportunities available to family members. The family also plays an important although not always visible role with respect to work—that is, families sustain and support the currently working members and create and raise new generations of workers.

Second, the stratification of families is not just a hierarchy of income or prestige; rather, families are linked to one another through the economic system that produces them. The linkage may be obscured by spatial separation, such as geographically or economically distinct neighborhoods, or the linkage may be direct, as when one family contracts for the labor of another. In both cases the linkage is simultaneously a product of and a precondition for the stratification of work and families.

Third, the relationship between work and family is dynamic and historically conditioned. As new systems of work (and, in general, new economic relations) have developed, they have caused massive changes in family structure. One need only contemplate the dramatic shifts in family structure occasioned by the transition from rural, agrarian economies to urban, industrial systems to recognize their importance: the separation of production from consumption, rendering families largely dependent on the labors of one (or possibly two) members; the lessening importance of inherited land or skills as a basis for continuity in economic activity; and the creation of external institutions and enterprises to provide basic services that were once handled within the family (education, childcare, the provision of clothing, emergency support, and so forth). Families have proven remarkably adaptable in responding to the transformation of economic systems. As might be expected, families in the 1980s are quite different from their eighteenth- and nineteenth-century predecessors, and, when considered across strata, they are very different from one another. Therefore, instead of assuming the family to be a universal category of social life, it is necessary to examine how the structure and internal operation of families differ over time and by economic position.

Fourth, even though popular use of the term *family* incorrectly specifies different social forms (historically and hierarchically), the term nonetheless has substantial normative and ideological influence. The "war over the family," as it has recently been called (Berger and Berger, 1983), is a direct reflection of the tension between the economic (and racial) stratification of families and the ideological influence of a universal notion of the proper, or "normal," family. Families without the economic resources to provide enough food, shelter, education, or financial security for their offspring are found lacking when compared to a "normal" family. Whether the blame for this situation is assigned to society, the economy, or to the family itself depends on the political stance of the observer. What unites those with different political ideologies, however, is a broad faith in the moral, religious, psychological, and social benefits of a family form that is striking in its similarity to the middle-class norm: the husband and wife residing with and providing for their children in a self-sufficient manner. Unstable, low-paying jobs create stress for poor families (particularly because families are actively judged by those in positions of social influence); but the abundance of work and high rewards for career commitment create tension for the dual-career couple as well. Most important are the problems couples encounter as they seek to mold family life to work demands without either violating norms that concern spousal roles, childcare, and household management *or* falling short of employers' expectations about vocational commitment and work performance.

Although it may occupy a special and contingent, or privileged, position in the stratification of families, the dual-career marriage nonetheless poses an important contrast to other family forms, and as such it raises two sets of core questions about the sociology of work and family. The first set considers the impact of work on the family: What effect do husbands' and wives' work-related lives have on the social structure of the family and on gender roles? Will the attainment of equal economic status by husbands and wives lead to an egalitarian division of labor and authority in the household? What effect does the "marriage" of two careers have on individual career strategies?

The second set of questions considers the impact of the family on the workplace: What effect does the dual-career family form have on individuals' expectations about work and the responsiveness of employing firms to changing family structures? Do these couples make new demands on their employers to adjust to the needs of a two-career family? Both sets of questions constitute the basis for this study.

## RESEARCH ON DUAL-CAREER FAMILIES

In analyzing the relationship between work and family, this study draws on the insights of two bodies of literature: the limited but influential research conducted in recent years on dual-career families, and the broader and somewhat more expansive literature on corporate careers.

The literature on dual-career families, most notably the works by Rapoport and Rapoport (1971, 1976), Hunt and Hunt (1977), Holmstrom (1973), and Bird (1979), has offered important insights on the specific impacts of work on family.[3] In particular, the Rapoports' case histories and the Hunts' articles have highlighted the difficulties husbands and wives face in adjusting home life to the demands of two jobs.

There is no clear-cut agreement by researchers on whether joining two careers in one family leads to a substantial change in family structure or gender roles. The Rapoports (1971, 1976), for example, conclude that the dual-career marriage has the potential for greater

3. Although *Tradeoffs* by Greiff and Munter (1979) and *The Two-Career Couple* by Hall and Hall (1979) have received considerable attention, both works tend to emphasize coping strategies for working couples and draw on prior research for their recommendations, rather than providing an analysis of original data.

equality in task performance and in responsibility for each spouse.[4] They base their conclusion on direct investigations of the division of labor in dual-career families, which found that husbands had assumed greater responsibility for household chores and childcare. Other researchers have reported similar findings (Dizard, 1968; Garland, 1972; Miller, 1972; and Bailyn, 1970).[5]

A contending group of researchers, however, questions whether husbands' participation in wives' traditional domains (housekeeping and childcare) has, in fact, increased and, if so, what impact these changes have had on family structure or gender roles. Weingarten (1978), for example, found that although couples negotiated a division of labor that allowed wives to compensate for the time they spent away from the home, men chose not to do housework because it threatened their masculinity. Chores may have been reallocated and women released from certain responsibilities, but the gender roles implicit in the marriage relationship basically remained unaltered. In a study of female academic professionals, Yogev (1981) found that the women themselves did not want to change the traditional aspects of their lives; that is, they continued to assume most of the responsibilities for childcare and housework. Yet, these women perceived themselves and their husbands as

4. The Hunts' research (1977) is also in accord with these findings, but they contend that the connection between careers and marriage may be a moot issue, since in their estimation the dual-career couple will remain a relatively small proportion of the range of family forms. Unlike the Hunts, however, I see the dual-career family as something of a laboratory for examining the impact of career on family, and therefore I feel it is worthwhile to extrapolate from these couples' experiences—even if they are numerically few.

5. In a recent addition to the literature on dual-career couples, Gerstel and Gross (1984) point out that in commuter marriages (that is, where husbands and wives work in different cities and maintain two residences) there is greater equality in household responsibilities and family authority. These couples, a subset of the general category of dual-career couples, demonstrate a remarkable adaptability to career demands.

equals. Yogev concludes that these women were undergoing role expansion (adding new responsibilities without relinquishing old ones) rather than role redefinition. Going even further, Perrucci et al. (1978), Bryson et al. (1978), Poloma and Garland (1971), Bird (1979), and Pleck (1977)[6] suggest that some of the more optimistic findings about equality within couples were illusory and that couples tended to exhibit a traditional division of labor even as they endured the combined pressures of two careers. Moreover, as Bird (1979) found, wives were often saddled with a double-duty day: their work outside the home resulted in rescheduling, rather than reduction, of traditional household chores.

Holmstrom's (1973) research serves as an important bridge between the two contending views. As in the work of the Rapoports and others, Holmstrom charted the emergence of new household and childcare arrangements between husbands and wives. Some couples, with the help of husbands or hired workers, were able to release wives from their traditional duties. However, Holmstrom also found that

> relative to men—specifically their husbands—the professional women fare less well. Despite their great deviation from middle-class norms, most professional couples were still a great distance from equality of the sexes. Even though both careers were important, typically the man's career was still more important. . . . The woman's time—although valuable—was less valuable than the man's. . . . And on the domestic side equality was also lacking. No matter how much help the woman received, the domestic realm was defined ultimately as her responsibility; it was

6. The research conducted by both Pleck and Bird involved a mix of dual-career and dual-job couples. The differences between jobs and careers—particularly in the income generated and the time demands required—are important and will be considered in the next section.

> ultimately not defined as a responsibility to be shared equally by both spouses (155).

Thus, she concludes, a career for a married woman may have helped diminish slightly the extent of inequality associated with marital roles; yet, at root, her status as a woman and as a wife continues to act as a major obstacle to marital equality.

My study, conducted over a decade after Holmstrom's, finds a revolution of sorts occurring within a similar stratum of couples. In contrast to the rather thinly veiled traditionalism of marital roles among Holmstrom's couples, the couples in this study demonstrated a markedly greater degree of equality in terms of household chores, marital decision making, and career evaluation (these findings are elaborated in chapters 2 through 5). As the two groups of women interviewed were approximately the same ages and were all well invested in their careers, some factor that accounts for this difference must have affected the marital process of negotiation and role definition. The key factor, I believe, is the decade separating the couples, a decade in which the women's movement evolved an ideology broad enough to encompass the marital and job experiences of middle-class women. Even though the men and women in my study only rarely make a direct causal link between their present situation and the ideology of the women's movement, I suggest that the movement helped legitimate careers for women and thus made possible (but did not cause) a "revolution" in marital roles and marital process.

In this study I share with prior researchers of dual-career couples a concern for detailing the impact of work on family life, household structure, and gender roles, although my work differs from others in two important respects. First, unlike the work of the Rapoports, Holmstrom, Bird, and others, this study is devoted exclusively to the study of dual-*career* couples in *corporate* organizations. Having a career instead of a job is an important difference. Those who pursue careers are generally well educated, well paid, ambitious, and, most important, committed to a structure that is well defined and controlled by a hierarchy of superiors. Unlike the lawyers, doctors, and college professors who predominated in the samples interviewed by the Rapoports, Holmstrom, and Gerstel and Gross, the couples interviewed for this book do not have such "transportable" careers. These individuals tend to be committed, at least in the beginning through the middle years of their employment, to a corporation that expects devotion to specific, externally derived objectives and also, if necessary, willingness to move organizationally or geographically. These couples lack the mobility enjoyed by many other professionals, and thus they lack the degree of freedom other professional couples may have in adjusting work to family and vice versa. Unlike the jobholders among Bird's two-paycheck couples, each spouse has a career, and the income and satisfaction derived from work (especially the wife's) is deemed essential to the couple. Her career, in particular, is neither temporary nor fixed in duration, and the couple's budget is predicated on her continuing (and increasing) income.

Second, the couples in this study represent the broader category of dual-career couples of which Gerstel and Gross's long-distance commuters are a subset. Although some of the couples I interviewed have experienced or contemplated long-distance commuting, in general they are a more representative sample of dual-career couples in the corporate world. Although census figures are insufficient to provide a precise empirical judgment, it is reasonable to assume that the percentage of dual-career couples living and working in the same geographical area (particularly in major metropolitan centers) far outnumbers those who commute.

This study is thus unique in its focus on the marriage of two viable and similarly structured careers. Because corporate careers and their impact on the family are central concerns, it also provides the opportunity to generate useful insights for the sociology of work and occupations, particularly for that segment dealing with corporate careers.

## BEYOND ORGANIZATION MEN AND TOKEN WOMEN

Among sociological analyses that have considered the intersection of career and family, two are particularly relevant here: William H. Whyte's *The Organization Man* (1956) and Rosabeth Kanter's *Men and Women of the Corporation* (1977). Both Whyte and Kanter were primarily interested in the organization of corporations and the interface between the individual employee and the organization; thus they consider family an appendage—something that involves the individual outside of the corporation.

Whyte reveals that the organization man not only reflected the corporate image but also enhanced a particular image of corporate America during the 1950s. Organization men were hardworking, churchgoing family heads; wives were corporate ambassadors who furthered the firm's standing in the immediate locale. Whyte focuses attention on the family, and particularly on relations between husbands and wives, as a way of showing how corporate policy and practice affected it.

He shows, for example, how the behavior, lifestyle, and activities of corporate wives were largely determined by their husbands' work positions and aspirations (Whyte 1951, 1952).

Kanter also places spouses (including the husbands of corporate women) largely outside the organization. This emphasis in Kanter's work derives from one of her principal arguments, that organizations construct the behavior, attitudes, and aspirations of organizational participants. In her effort to downplay the effect of imported or sex-linked attitudes and behaviors, especially those commonly believed to distinguish male and female corporate employees, Kanter places the greatest emphasis on the relationship between the organization's structure and purpose and the individual. Women highly placed within organizational hierarchies are often "tokens" in groups numerically dominated by men, for example, and this token status may shape behavior and interaction between men and women in work groups. Kanter contends, however, that wives are major, if often invisible, social actors in the corporate organization and in the structure of their husbands' corporate careers. She points out that although wives do not "appear" important because their roles are played outside the day-to-day corporate milieu, a wife's social position is in fact quite important for a husband's status and prestige in the world and for his social position (and likelihood of promotion) within the corporation. Kanter convincingly argues that wives are the second person in a "two-person career" within the corporate organization itself (see also Papanek, 1975). Although Kanter includes the wife as a category within the corporation, by ignoring or not taking into account those families that have invested in two separate careers, she represents the wife's organizational role as specific and limited. In contrast, this study confronts issues that concern family organization and family relationships under conditions in which the wife is not invisible but is instead capable of making direct claims on her husband and her husband's career. I have attempted to go beyond the two-person career in order to assess the impact of the *two-career person,* that is, the individual who must take into account not only his or her own career concerns but also those of the spouse.

## FROM FAMILY TO WORK

As we enter the late 1980s, a question has arisen as to whether family should remain outside the realm of organizational careers. With the trend toward greater participation by women in corporate employment and careers (beyond "tokenism" as described by Kanter and others), the relationship between corporation, individual, and family takes on new importance. How might the greater possibilities and the demand for women to have equal access to careers and commensurate economic rewards affect the structure of work organizations? Conversely, if women and perhaps men desire career success as well as family commitments, can we then expect a lessening or even a reversal in the influence of work on family? Will the family act to structure careers within the corporation?

These questions begin where Whyte's and Kanter's pathbreaking analyses left off. Whyte's *Organization Man* accurately portrayed the organizational world of the 1950s and 1960s, where men completely dominated managerial and professional positions in corporations and where the cloistered existence of wives and families was clearly subordinate to the husbands' organizational life; a cultural feature of the 1950s was the wife who acted as a backdrop to her husband's career. Kanter's study, which covered the late 1960s through the mid-1970s, not only detailed the emergence of a real transition in the gender composition of the corporate labor force but also sought to explain how women were utilized by their corporate employers. Kanter was concerned, at least in part, with the daughters of Whyte's organization men.

Although my own study is not based on a clear historical break, such as the one that distinguishes Whyte's from Kanter's work, it focuses on further implications of the trend Kanter noted. Whereas Kanter highlighted the movement of women into "men's" careers and sought to make sense of women's relationships to their male counterparts in male-dominated organizations, this book assumes that women have already blazed trails into the corporate domain and that, although their roles and career prospects are still being defined, they have achieved sufficient permanence and stability in their careers to make their positions, behaviors, and expectations about family, marriage, and children increasingly significant. Unless corporate women have decided not to have children (an assumption contradicted by my data), family considerations must directly enter their calculations about occupational choice and career trajectory and must have at least some influence on how organizations themselves operate.

Precisely how this influence is manifested is one of the central issues of this study. In approaching this question, it is important to recognize how both males and females who pursue careers confront the organizations that employ them. Quite simply, dual-career couples, as well as the larger category of females with careers, confront their corporate employers more on an individual basis than as a consciously integrated group. Because the corporation is a white-collar work environment, where advancement is predicated on competition with peers and performance is measured individually, employees are forced to deal with the company as individuals. Although in some areas of white-collar work—particularly the lower echelons, which contain dead-end positions such as clerical jobs—a measure of solidarity may develop in the face of corporate management, career employees are encouraged to define themselves as individuals and to solve problems, even recurrent, similar problems, individually. The corporate emphasis on contributing to the achievement of organizational goals directly diminishes the possibility of placing individual (or family) needs first.

The hegemony of corporate needs is completed by the active recruitment of the employees' own consent to subordinate their individual concerns. Gerstel and Gross (1984) hit the nail on the head when they argue that

> the insensitivity [to private concerns] is not limited to employers who maintain long-standing traditions. Professionals themselves are caught in a logic of careers and a culture that demands the dominance of work (200–201).

Career employees are caught in a bind in two ways. First, they must place a high priority on work in order to achieve economic rewards and social status for themselves and their families. Second, like all those whose present success appears linked to past sacrifice (personal or familial), they are sorely tempted to redefine that sacrifice at best as a badge of honor and at worst as a necessary evil. In both instances, successful pursuit of an individual goal is explicitly and implicitly tied to the achievement of an overriding organizational purpose.

For dual-career couples to truly increase their influence over employers, the organization's objective and subjective dominance must be undermined. If the logic of careers and the culture of work pervade all aspects of social life, then the relationship between economic organizations and those who pursue careers within them is akin to that of magician and audience. The essence of magic is misdirection—focusing the observer's attention where the action is not in order to disguise the act itself. By attending to the misdirection, the audience participates in the act, whether or not it really believes in magic.

The objective circumstances of dual-career couples—their combined career demands in conflict with family responsibilities and desires—may lead them to chafe under the conditions that organizations impose. But whether they will actively question corporate dominance (the magic) and then demand change (expose the misdirection) remains at issue.

## AT THE CROSSROADS: A NEW MARITAL BOND?

In addition to analyzing the impacts of work on family and family on work, I hope to focus attention on another, perhaps more fundamental, question: do the social and economic changes that have made the dual-career marriage possible require the creation of a new marital bond? This question arises from both the unique circumstances of the dual-career marriage and the mythical character it has assumed in recent years. In other words, when marriage is shorn of wives' traditional economic dependence on husbands, what will hold the family together? If both husbands and wives work in rewarding careers that neither is willing to sacrifice, and if neither is given the exclusive title of breadwinner (or homemaker, for that matter), what happens to authority in the family? And what happens to the gender roles associated with husband and wife and to the subtle yet powerful underpinnings of the marital bond?

The dual-career marriage represents, albeit on a limited scale, what feminists called for in the 1960s and 1970s: a relationship unfettered by the dominance of economically "productive" men over their economically "unproductive" wives. In an effort to assess whether, in fact, dual careers substantially affect this marital bond, I will pay close attention to the implications of economic independence for the material as well as the psychological basis of marriage.

## ORGANIZATION OF THE STUDY

Organizing this study was like trying to solve two puzzles at once, as I am simultaneously examining both the influence of work on family organization and the influence of family on work organization. To accomplish this dual goal, it is necessary to look at the *process* of dual-career couple development rather than simply its outcome. There is no master plan on the part of either work organizations or families to *consciously* influence each other. Instead, changes in work organizations, individual orientations toward careers, or family organizations are often only vaguely intentional. Couples feel their way through problems without the benefit of guidance from a well-defined set of rules and roles inherited from earlier generations. The majority of these couples did not grow up as the sons and daughters of dual-career couples, and thus they cannot look to their childhood family experiences to provide a framework of clues and memories for solving their daily problems. Their uncertainty about solutions reflects their own inexperience with this situation as much as it does the relative newness of the phenomenon for social science.

People are often tempted to view their own life courses as intentionally self-directed. Yet, when I invited these couples to describe their personal histories, without asking them to justify their current positions, their answers revealed the incremental and often quite uncertain process by which they arrived at their present situation. Over and over again, individuals ascribed success to luck. They believed luck explained their career accomplishments and their success in balancing work and family lives. Attributing the hard work of balancing two careers, a household, and, in some instances, children to luck does not explain how many vexing problems were solved. Moreover, it denies that problems exist or existed in the past.

Solutions, even temporary ones, to the problem of weaving together public and private lives are most often arrived at by a series of guesses or by imitating examples of others in similar situations—such "pioneers" as the handful of friends or acquaintances or people these couples have read about. How Joan Franklin from the New York office solved a problem with her housekeeper when the schedule conflicted with an overseas assignment becomes folklore in the Chicago office in a matter of days. Like nervous brokers on Wall Street, these couples are constantly alert to any tidbits of information that might apply to their situation.

Ferreting out information and discovering pioneers only addresses part of the problem. What remains difficult, and perhaps most important, is establishing a fair and reliable way of balancing the demands of work and family. Even the "well-informed" couple must still cope with unpredictable requests from two employers, make investment decisions regarding education and technical skills, arrange a household, achieve some measure of intimacy, and, in many cases, struggle with the questions of whether to have children and how to raise them. Husbands and wives in dual-career situations must *negotiate* many aspects of their individual and communal lives.

In order to analyze the relationship between work and family and to understand how the dual-career couple operates, it is necessary to probe deeply into the details of their work and family lives and into the means and parameters of their short- and long-term negotiations. Investigation of both process and outcome is necessary if we are to understand what factors are heavily weighted (career, salary, finances, children) and how they are prioritized. For these reasons and because the dual-career couple is a relatively new phenomenon, I employed a more qualitative emphasis in data collection. A larger survey would have increased the sample size, but it would have allowed fewer questions and only restricted opportunities for probing beyond superficial responses. Instead, data collection consisted primarily of semi-structured, depth interviews with both husbands and wives of dual-career couples. The semi-structured format allowed respondents to be questioned in detail about their attitudes and behaviors regarding work and family, individual work histories, work relationships, family and personal finances, and household issues. Husbands and wives in these couples were interviewed separately, making it possible to gather information without direct concern about effects caused by the spouse's presence. This approach also allowed both factual and attitudinal data to be cross-checked between spouses.

A total of twenty-one dual-career couples were interviewed, which translated into a total of forty-two interviews averaging two-and-a-half hours each. Some respondents were reinterviewed in order to fill in gaps or to answer further questions. All the interviews were tape recorded, with the permission of the respondents, and additional notes were taken at the time of the interviews. The interviews were subsequently transcribed and coded for data analysis. All respondents were guaranteed anonymity, and names have been changed in the text to protect the identities of participants, their families, and their employers.

Participants in this study were selected from a pool of couples identified by informants in corporations located in the Chicago metropolitan area. Because there is no easy way to identify dual-career couples, it is difficult to speak about these couples as being directly representative of all dual-career couples. However, efforts were made to select respondents so as to minimize variability in careers and maximize variability in family situations.

The sample represents a cross section of those dual-career couples who could be identified through knowledgeable informants. (See Table 1 for characteristics of the sample.) Three factors were important in the sampling procedure: (1) each individual (male and female) had a position at the middle-management level or above or an established position in a profession;[7] (2) both couples with children and couples without children were included; and (3) cases in which husbands earned more than their wives, the same as their wives, or less than their wives were all included. This final point was intended to allow investigation into issues of income level and authority within the family.

I was also concerned that this sample reflect the role

7. My concern was to identify people in corporate managerial careers, rather than those in individual professions with noncorporate affiliations.

TABLE 1. Selected Characteristics of the Sample

| | *Male* | *Female* |
|---|---|---|
| Median age | 36.3 | 34.3 |
| (standard deviation) | (4.0) | (3.1) |
| (minimum/maximum) | (29/45) | (28/38) |
| Median individual income | $47,500 | $40,200 |
| (standard deviation) | ($20,017) | ($18,806) |
| (minimum/maximum) | ($21,000/$90,000) | ($18,000/$100,000) |
| Median joint income | $90,250 | |
| (standard deviation) | ($26,743) | |
| (minimum/maximum) | ($48,000/$142,000) | |
| Median years married (in present marriage) | 9.0[a] | |
| (standard deviation) | (4.1) | |
| (minimum/maximum) | (4/14) | |
| Residence (% urban) | 71.4% | |

NOTE: All respondents were Caucasian.

[a]Of the forty-two people in the sample, seven had been married prior to their current marriage. Only two of these seven had been married to someone else longer than to their current spouse; these same two were the only people in the sample who had children from an earlier marriage.

of large-scale firms as trendsetters in the organization and trajectory of careers. Where possible, couples were therefore selected if at least one spouse was employed by a large corporation. Firms represented in the sample included major financial, consulting, industrial, and entertainment enterprises and ranged in profit levels from several million to several hundred million dollars annually. The work locales were principally in major regional or national headquarters. (See the Appendix for more detail.)

Another significant characteristic of this sample is that the couples I interviewed were not involved in new or young marriages. As Table 1 shows, the median length of time these couples had been married was nine years. In effect, I have captured the lives of these people *after* the point at which daily living adjustments were made.

Findings from this study are presented through an examination of the general issues facing dual-career couples, beginning in Chapter 2 with a consideration of work life and careers for men and women in the modern corporation—how individuals arrived at their present positions, the significance careers have to these individuals, and the implications of two careers in a family for individual career decisions. Chapter 3 marks a transition from specific concerns about work to the implications of work, and particularly of income, for the internal organization of a family. Although money does make a difference in distinguishing these couples from most other couples, money alone is not enough to resolve issues of power and equity between husbands and wives. Chapter 4 explores the most private of family decisions—having or not having children—and considers its public consequences and political nature. Chapter 5 analyzes how children are integrated into the dual-career family and suggests that the private matter of how to raise children, as well as the initial decision about having them, can only be understood within the context of work and the larger system of economic stratification. Chapter 6 brings the pieces of the puzzle together by focusing on the relationship between career and family as it is worked out in the dual-career marriage. The study concludes by presenting proposals for a broader theoretical model of family, work, and gender roles.

## CONCLUSION

Although dual-career couples may be relatively few in number, they are nevertheless important to study. Even if they have the economic wherewithal for the lifestyle depicted in subsequent chapters, the glamorous image presented by the media does not capture the contradictions and conflicts generated by the competing demands of work and family. One often assumes that money (or resources) can solve the problems of most of the less advantaged groups in our society. But the problem is not that simple. To what extent have these couples had to struggle to piece together the public and private sides of their lives? Even those with resources face problems that are unresolved, given the present structure of work organizations. And, more important, these problems cannot be solved in isolation.

The couples presented here have painstakingly attempted to combine their work lives with families. Yet even for this fortunate group of fortunate couples, "having it all" has had its costs. Listening to them reveals a great deal about the uphill fight couples wage when they try to avoid being trapped in the traditional social and cultural definitions of family and of women's and men's work.

This study adds fuel to the argument that the "personal is political." The point of the women's movement in the 1960s and 1970s was not simply to pit each woman in a struggle against her man behind closed doors. The purpose of sexual politics was to make public the personal problems that women had faced in isolation. For the generation of women who have had the opportunity to have careers (and, for that matter, for their husbands), it is essential to bring to the forefront the new problems that go along with having it all—including the personal problems these individuals are afraid to voice collectively to their employers for fear of individual and perhaps collective reprisal.

Finally, I hope to raise a parallel question: does the corporation have the right to ask people to sacrifice their personal lives to advance corporate goals and profits? Put differently, how much of a person's blood, sweat, and tears do employers have a right to expect? The concept of commitment has been a central issue in studies of work and occupations. But have we perhaps carried this notion too far?

# 2

# THREE CAREERS: His Work, Her Work, and Their Marriage

ALL MARRIAGES are shaped by work. Work determines a family's standard of living, its status with respect to other families, and, to some extent, the life chances or opportunities of its individual members. But equally important, the division of labor inside a family mirrors the distinction between husbands, who traditionally supported the family economically, and wives, who worked in the home, by extension making it possible for husbands to continue to work. Even though the two systems support each other, it does not necessarily follow that they are equivalent or equally valued socially; nor does it follow that the social roles of breadwinner and homemaker are equally valued. In fact, work and family are seen as separate and noncomparable spheres of activity, and the social and economic valuations of breadwinning/breadwinners and homemaking/homemakers remain quite different.

Higher social status has been attached to work in the economic sphere than to work in the home, and those family members active as wage earners have thus tended to exercise authority based on their higher status. The traditional nuclear family represents the conjoining of two distinct activities with distinctly unequal statuses, mirroring both the system of social stratification based on economic roles and the system of gender stratification that has grown up beside economic inequality. In the family, the social roles of husband and wife and the gender roles of men and women are integrated. Husbands exercise authority over wives by virtue of their higher social status as economic actors, and men exercise authority over women by virtue of their roles as husbands and patriarchs.

Yet, this description of the relationship between work and family is far from complete. Although men derive higher status from being economically active and use that status to exercise authority over their wives, they nonetheless are dependent on their wives and families to provide the physical support necessary to continue working (meals, clean clothes, a household) and the psychological and emotional support necessary to withstand the demands of work. Thus, work confers authority on men in the family, but family (and particularly the wife's role) contributes heavily to their ability to work. The subordinate position of wife makes women economically dependent on their husbands, but the core activities of homemaking create a sphere in which women perform roles critical to the husband's position outside the home. In effect, through marriage a wife becomes economically dependent on a husband, and he becomes emotionally dependent on her.[1]

More concretely, the particular job he occupies determines how much time and which specific periods of

1. For a similar argument about how the economic independence of men has been mistaken for emotional independence, see Rubin (1983) and Chapter 4. For literature on the differential effects of marriage for men and women, see Helsing et al. (1981) and Bernard (1973).

time the husband spends with his wife and children. If his job entails a great deal of travel, he might be away for days with no family contact beyond a nightly phone call. If he works the night shift, he may see his children after school but rarely in the evenings. If his work is seasonal, he will be unavailable to family members during certain months of the year and at home twenty-four hours a day during other months. And whereas the wife may be able to schedule family outings, tickets to the theater, dinner parties—all aspects of their social life together—around his work schedule, unpredictable events are hers to handle alone: the boiler blows up, a child requires an emergency appendectomy, a mother is taken ill, and so on. In short, a husband's participation in family life is restricted to the hours he is not at work, whereas a wife keeps a twenty-four-hour vigil over family life.

## THE DUAL-CAREER CHALLENGE

The dual-career marriage challenges a number of principles of the traditional marriage. Work and its rewards still shape a couple's life chances; but instead of a single career or job defining marital roles, there are two careers, qualifying each spouse as a breadwinner. Many dual-career couples live better than their more traditional counterparts, but ambiguity and confusion surround the marriage of two careers: no one partner can claim authority in the household based on "bringing home the bacon." Questions of whose work and time commitments should take precedence are muddied by similar and competing employer demands; arriving at a division of labor for household tasks is complicated by both spouses' daytime absence from the home. Traditional corporate careers required that the husband as employee and the wife as his aide join forces in what Papanek (1975) referred to as the "two-person career." Dual-career marriages have two husbands and no wife.

Ambiguity and confusion about social roles is a common feature of the way people experience social change. People may only dimly perceive new expectations about behavior as new practices emerge; marital roles are no exception. What makes the experience of the dual-career couples in this study important is that their efforts to define a new set of roles *did not precede* the marriage. Rather, they struggled with role definitions only *after* the practical aspects of change began to emerge. Like a picture slowly brought into focus, the practical implications of change took time to appear as something comprehensible: a marriage as a relationship apart from, yet dependent on, their individual careers.

Groping for words to describe his dual-career marriage, one husband struck on what he felt was an apt metaphor:

> It's two separate lives in some ways. It's like a dual carriageway, and we are both going down those carriageways at more or less the same speed, I would say. While those carriageways don't cross one another, if something happens on one of them, something necessarily happens on the other one.

His metaphor is suggestive: it implies a distinctness of careers for the partners in the marriage. Yet it does not explain how or why a change in one affects the other. This ambiguity in describing the linkage between the two careers is not, however, simply the product of a faulty metaphor. Rather, it reflects a general inability on the part of these couples to accurately describe how their careers are related, how they came to choose those careers, and, most important, how they came to mesh and manage two careers in one marriage.

Without many models to use as benchmarks, dual-career couples tend to measure themselves against the traditional roles of husband and wife, models that provide often insufficient and contradictory advice regarding these couples' situations. However, these couples have not simply benefited from a felicitous combination of good planning and good luck. Such a conclusion overlooks the consolidation of *three* careers in the dual-career marriage: his, hers, and theirs. The marriage is the "third career," which bears remarkable similarities to a career in the work world, especially in a new industry. For example, everyone knows the title of "manager," but few have a clear sense when they embark on a career just what "managing" entails and just where they will end up—though, of course, everyone has plans. Career marriages are similar; in addition to wanting to be a husband or wife, each member has to comprehend and work at that role as it emerges over time.

The third career (the marriage) is "made," not imitated or automatically acquired, and therefore it involves confusion and uncertainty. The couples' unease in dealing with an ambiguous situation creates frustration as they try to make a new reality fit an old model. Far from being the avant-garde of a social movement, with an articulate vision of what they want to create, these couples are notable for their lack of ideological prescriptions about the equality of marital roles. Instead, combining two equally demanding (and rewarding) careers, they simply practice such equality. Although rough edges remain to be smoothed, marital roles reflect many of the objectives espoused by many feminist theorists, even though neither spouse may have had prior indoctrination in the ideology of equality.

This chapter examines men's and women's careers—what they are and how they developed. Recounting the process of career building provides a means for considering the dynamics of building the third career, marriage. The exigencies of a career (travel, long hours) are difficult enough to juggle for one individual with a career; the joint exigencies become even more difficult to handle when there are two careers; with three careers, the situation becomes exponentially more problematic. The second section of this chapter deals directly with dual-career couples' marriages, using detailed data from interviews to analyze how career demands and commitment to marriage interact to create both practical devices for coping and challenges to the ideology of the traditional family.[2]

2. Each respondent was asked to detail his or her career history and then to locate the timing of marriage within that history. Of the forty-two respondents, seven had been married once before, but at different points in their career history and (in the case of the four men) to spouses without careers. (Both husband and wife in two couples had been divorced previously; thus a total of five marriages involved either spouse having been divorced.) Data used in this study are drawn from couples' current marriages only.

Three of the four previously married men remarried women who were already involved in careers. Although all three women who had been married previously worked during their first marriages, two married their first and second husbands before beginning careers, and one had a career already underway when she married her first husband. Thus, only one woman in this group of seven had a first marriage described as being dual-career.

Only two of these seven individuals had been married to someone else longer than to their present spouse; these two men are the only people in the sample to have children from their earlier marriage. The remaining five individuals had been married to their first spouse less than three years.

I did not question any of these individuals at length about their first marriages, although I did ask why the first marriages ended and if the ending had been work-related. Only one man noted a work connection, describing himself as a "workaholic," a tendency he has tried to curb in his present marriage, although he believes that his present wife doesn't mind as much because she has her own career. The woman who had a dual-career first marriage stated that being at similar career stages and in the same field had produced fierce competition between her and her first husband. She remarried a man ten years her senior. Remaining respondents cited the spouse's troublesome daily habits or extramarital affairs as reasons for divorce. I did

## WHAT THEY DO: A SAMPLING

Work in the corporate white-collar world may not be as muscle-straining or as dangerous as mining, steelmaking, or automobile assembly, but it has its costs. Sixty- and seventy-hour workweeks are not uncommon; ulcers, fatigue, and stress are frequent complaints. Free time usually evaporates in the heat of deadlines, hurried projects, organizational crises, and, in many positions, incessant demands for travel (to meet clients, put out fires in distant field offices, or start a new position in the organization).

Simply getting things done is often difficult enough; getting ahead requires help from all quarters. In the 1950s and 1960s white-collar world described by Whyte (1956), an executive wife maintained the home and acted as a backstop for her husband's career. Her contribution, although receiving minimal social recognition, was a real one. For dual-career couples, the demands on family are doubled. Indeed, given the cyclical character of work scheduling in some industries, the demands can be tripled, as might be the case for a husband and wife who are both tax accountants and thus busiest at one time of the year.

The financial rewards for corporate work are, of course, significantly better than those received by miners, steelworkers, or autoworkers. Money, perquisites, prestige, and power induce (or, as many of my interviewees suggested, seduce) the career-oriented individual to give up time, energy, and often family life to meet organizational demands. Once a person is on the career trail,

---

examine whether divorce was related to type of accounting system, and I asked if financial arrangements in current marriages were the same as in first marriages, although this sample of remarried individuals is too small to allow any conclusions about whether or not people do things differently the second time around. None of these individuals were receiving alimony from or paying alimony to their first spouses.

however, financial rewards serve as much to extract commitment as to induce it. Most individuals find it difficult to contemplate, much less to risk, a substantial reduction in earnings in order to move out of an organization or a line of work they find unsatisfying. Dual-career couples enjoy the benefits of two sizeable incomes, and the combined earnings and the lifestyle they generate are difficult to ignore or to risk.

On the way up the career ladder, strain and sizeable savings accounts, along with constant work demands and expensive "restorative" vacations, become the double binds tying each person to his or her career. With each promotion comes more organizational responsibility and further personal investment in the organization.

At the time these men and women were interviewed, they had been in their present place of employment for at least three years. The majority affirmed that there was room for upward mobility in their corporations. Although all occupied positions at the level of manager or above, their responsibilities and specialties were diverse. To give some sense of these people and their work, I will briefly describe three couples.

### *Two Vice-Presidents*

At age thirty-four, Jenny is vice-president for corporate development and strategic planning for a Chicago-based corporation with nine operating companies. She is responsible for reviewing the operating companies' earnings forecasts and strategic plans. Jenny and an economic analyst on her staff create and revise models forecasting the companies' financial performance—assessing and devising ways to improve returns on capital. She regularly attends budget and planning meetings for the operating companies and consults with those units' presidents each month. These responsibilities occasionally require her to make day trips outside the city. She reports to a higher-level executive and routinely participates in meetings on overall business strategy. Recent moves by the parent corporation into new commodity markets have caused her to extend her forecasting responsibilities to this area as well. Rarely home before 7:30 P.M. on weekdays and often obliged to work Saturdays, Jenny earns $40,000 a year.

Her husband, Tony, at thirty-seven is a vice-president for personnel administration in a financial services corporation. He directly oversees a staff of twenty-five people and reports to a senior vice-president. His responsibilities include the administration of payroll, compensation programs, and fringe benefits, as well as the procurement and training of clerical, accounting, data processing, and security personnel. Tony also spends part of his time on projects related to fringe benefit and compensation programs, in particular, assessing data and making comparisons with similarly situated companies. On occasion he does general personnel work and is also called on to lend a hand in the operations area, where he had his last assignment. Tony's work often keeps him in the office past 7:00 P.M. He earns $45,000 a year.

Jenny and Tony live in a striking two-floor condominium in a fashionable Chicago neighborhood. They have been married for thirteen years and have a three-year-old child.

### *Corporate Lawyer and Consulting Manager*

Sam is a thirty-four-year-old lawyer for a major utility company. He handles the legal aspects of the company's oil and natural gas operations. Most of his work involves implementing transactions that have originated elsewhere in the corporation, and it requires his considerable technical knowledge to prepare and file registration statements for securities. Sam travels an average of 25 percent of the year. For instance, during one recent month he spent every other week in Canada working on a financial deal for the company. A few months later he alternated between London and Chicago for a stretch of eight weeks. The periods of time between trips were interspersed with overnight trips to New York and San Francisco. When in town, he normally leaves the office between 7:00 and 9:00 P.M. each evening. He earns $58,000 a year.

Linda, Sam's thirty-year-old wife, is a manager in a major business consulting firm. The firm's clients include both domestic and international corporations. Linda works as an engagement manager with a team of professionals on projects that usually last three to four months. Her responsibility is to ride herd on the project team and to make sure its analysis is appropriately targeted and that the problems it identifies are well defined. She is a principal contact for clients and remains in constant (sometimes daily) communication with them as a project progresses. Time demands vary with the life cycle of each project. Initial encounters and site visits with clients can be exhausting; when a project settles down, however, she can trim her workday to eight or nine hours. Completing a project often requires a return to fifteen- and sixteen-hour days. Linda travels roughly one-third of the year; depending on the nature of the project, her time away from home can vary from two days to a month at a time. She earns $53,000 a year.

Sam and Linda live in a condominium they are restoring in the city. They have been married for five years, and although they have no children yet, they plan to have a child when, as Linda remarked, "they have time." Until then, work postpones the decision.

### *Marketing Director and Bank Vice-President*

Michelle, at thirty-six years old, is the director of marketing for the tourism and leisure division of a major publishing company. Her responsibilities include advertising and public relations for the company's resort hotels. In addition, she works with two outside advertising agencies and oversees all advertising budgets for the division. Michelle's position requires concern with every aspect of the resort hotels, from correspondence to press releases. Because her work crosses over into public relations, she must frequently travel to the disparately located foreign and domestic hotels and entertain guests, public officials, and the press for periods of up to three nights a week. She earns $40,000 a year.

John, her thirty-seven-year-old husband, is a vice-president for commercial lending at a major Chicago bank. For four days a week, his day begins with 8:30 A.M. meetings that may last from twenty minutes to three hours. He also meets daily with the three division heads who report to him; he in turn reports to the senior vice-president. In addition, he is commonly called in by the bank president to examine a complicated deal or to handle investment prospects unearthed by the chief executive. The remainder of his in-office day is devoted to handling clients, analyzing lending prospects, and evaluating the bank's financial profile. Lunches are usually spent dining or playing tennis with bank clients, prospective customers, or other officers. He describes his job as "jumping when you've got about ten other balls in the air at once." He earns $55,000 a year.

Married seven years, Michelle and John live in a large house in a North Shore suburb. They have one four-year-old child.

The couples described here are typical of the group I interviewed. Their combined incomes, by most standards, are impressive—but so are the demands they must fulfill to maintain them. To get a clearer sense of the careers—individual and joint—these couples are building, we must look closer at the larger sample. The sections that follow examine his, her, and their careers.

## CAREER BEGINNINGS: HIS CAREER

The men in this study grew up in the 1940s and early 1950s. For them, working was an expectation, not a choice. Their lives reflect the prototypical middle-class male career: college and graduate training, then a series of jobs. Their lives have followed a neat, orderly sequence. Fifty-two percent of the men went directly from college to graduate school. Another 24 percent went into the military after college graduation and then proceeded to graduate school. This man described the prototypical male career:

> I went to the University of Chicago, where I majored in economics and graduated in 1966. I went to the University of Chicago Business School immediately and graduated in 1968. So I entered the business world in 1968, and my first job was as a market analyst.

Many men prepared for careers through their choice of undergraduate majors (see Table 2). Unlike women, whose undergraduate majors are a bit more evenly distributed, almost two-thirds of the men majored in social

TABLE 2. Undergraduate Majors of Men and Women

| | *Women* | *Men* |
|---|---|---|
| Business | 19.0% (4) | 10.0% (2) |
| Journalism | 14.0% (3) | — (0) |
| Social science | 28.5% (6) | 62.0% (13) |
| Humanities | 28.5% (6) | 23.0% (5) |
| Sciences | 10.0% (2) | 5.0% (1) |

NOTE: N = 21 for both men and women.

science (specifically economics) and only a quarter majored in the humanities (specifically history).

Fifty-two percent of the men married when they graduated from college; in the majority of these cases, wives supported husbands while the latter earned advanced degrees. However, 48 percent of the men married after completing graduate education; typically, many of their wives were just completing college. In the first group, husbands and wives took turns going through graduate school, and in the second group, the husbands supported their wives through advanced training (see Table 3). At the time of these interviews, the men occupied as varied an array of positions in the Chicago business community as did the women. Table 4 outlines the positions the men occupied.

Changes in attitude about their role as breadwinners did not occur in the early part of these men's careers but rather took place more subtly as a result of their wives' entry into the labor market. The issue of how men's careers developed in tandem with their wives' careers and the consequent changes in the social roles of husband and wife will be discussed in a later section.

TABLE 3. Marriage and Advanced Education for Men

| *Postgraduate Degree* | *Married Before Completing Advanced Education* | *Married After Completing Advanced Education* |
|---|---|---|
| M.B.A. | 2 | 7 |
| J.D.–M.B.A. | 1 | 0 |
| M.D.–M.B.A. | 1 | 0 |
| M.A. (other nonbusiness) | 1 | 1 |
| J.D. | 3 | 2 |
| Total | 8 | 10 |

NOTE: Three men, not included in these figures, had only B.A.s. Two, however, had majored in business as undergraduates.

## CAREER BEGINNINGS: HER CAREER

"Caught in the middle"—between an old dream and a new reality—best describes the lives of the women interviewed in this study. Most graduated from college before 1972, the year in which the Senate passed the Equal Rights Amendment. These women were not "visionaries," activists in the women's movement, or, necessarily, adherents to feminist ideology, even when it became widespread. Few really had plans or thoughts about careers. Rather, most dreamed of fulfilling traditional roles as wives and mothers. Work was a way station on the road to realizing that dream. A white-collar job, even in management, was a temporary post to be superseded by marriage and children in the not-too-distant future.

The initial dreams of these women were largely indistinguishable from those of their female college-educated peers. They majored in a fairly broad array of disci-

TABLE 4. Organizational Positions and Activities of Dual-Career Husbands

| *Position/Title* | *Number* | *Associated Activities* |
|---|---|---|
| Vice-president | 5 | Personnel<br>Commercial lending<br>Marketing and communications |
| Manager | 8 | Finances<br>Sales<br>Loans<br>Advertising<br>Marketing |
| Professional | 5 | Corporate law<br>Medicine—health administration and health policy |
| Self-employed | 3 | Law<br>Consulting |
| Total | 21 | |

plines while in school; only four out of twenty-one concentrated in a business-related field (see Table 5). Most thought their degrees and college work experience would translate into employment, but none claimed that she had an early goal of the type of business career for which men trained. One woman, typical of the group, described her thoughts at the outset of her career:

> I was somewhat directionless and unfocused at that point. Chicago seemed as good a place to be as any, and my boyfriend was here. In 1966 it was relatively easy for women

with math and philosophy degrees to get good-paying jobs in data processing. The whole career start was accidental.

Another commented, "I didn't know what a C.P.A. was when I left school. I didn't have any idea that there was a profession identified by those initials. . . . As a teenager growing up, I never imagined being in business." All the women I interviewed worked after graduating from college; some drifted into potential career paths, while others found themselves in jobs. Two-thirds did not begin to pursue careers until some time after they were married.

Yet whatever their initial orientation, they belonged to a generation of women college graduates who were potential beneficiaries of an unprecedented opening of the labor market. Career opportunities were expanded as a result of politically mandated affirmative action programs and the broader campaign of the women's liberation movement. Corporate employers who did business with the federal government were compelled to demonstrate their willingness to recruit, train, and promote women. Other companies sought women to fill higher-level posi-

TABLE 5. Marriage and Undergraduate Majors for Women

| *Undergraduate Majors* | *Married Before Career Began* | *Married After Career Began* |
|---|---|---|
| Business | 2 | 2 |
| Journalism | 1 | 2 |
| Social science | 6 | 0 |
| Humanities | 4 | 2 |
| Sciences | 1 | 1 |
| Total | 14 | 7 |

tions for both real and symbolic purposes. Whatever the cause, the career possibilities for college-educated women increased. Many of the women I interviewed were thus well positioned to enter careers, even if they had not seriously considered doing so before.

Simply being at the right place at the right time, however, is not a sufficient explanation for these women's experiences, nor does it offer much insight into the role marriage played in the career-building process. Several instructive findings arose from an analysis of the interviews. First, few women moved directly into a career path before or after marriage. Contrary to the male prototype, women began with jobs, often quite heterogeneous, and slowly zeroed in on careers and organizations in which to pursue them. Second, the overwhelming majority of women, irrespective of the timing of career and marriage, found emotional support essential in making the transition from job to career. Finally, almost all of the women eventually convinced themselves, first, that they were not deviants among women or traitors to the prescription that women should primarily be wives and mothers and, second, that they were every bit as good as the men with whom they worked and competed (including, in some instances, their spouses). They had to engage in a personal process of demystification—of avoiding the magician's efforts at misdirection—in order to personally justify their positions, their relative success, and the changes their careers implied for marital roles.

The women who married before beginning careers married either before they finished college or shortly after receiving their college degrees. They married their college boyfriends or, in a few cases, high-school sweethearts. They married under the middle-class "rules" of the old dream, believing that once their husbands completed graduate school, they would assume their places as homemakers and wives. As one woman explained:

> At that point I really didn't have any long-term career goals. My goals had stopped when I graduated from college, and I hadn't really thought through what I intended to do after that. . . . Here I was with the thought that I was obviously going to get married and have children at a young age and do all those nice things that my mother did.

Neither their recountings nor their initial work histories indicate that these women held long-term career goals; instead, the question of employment was directly linked to their husbands' future work prospects. Wives' early work histories reflect husbands' career decisions. The following pattern was typical for many interviewees:

> I married a guy that I was madly in love with right after college. We both had degrees in journalism, but I followed him—his career. Every six months they would send him someplace else. So his first job was in Georgia, and I worked as a news editor for the *Dublin Herald*. . . . Six months later he got transferred to Chicago, and I followed him here and I got a job as a secretary at a TV studio; six months later he got transferred to Philadelphia . . . and I worked as an assistant director for an advertising agency.

When asked if these moves were discussed in any way, she continued:

> He would say, "We're moving," and I would say, "Fine, we're moving." He was pursuing his career, and I was just picking up whatever I could. I really had no idea what I wanted. I was not a driven person. I am what I am because of a lot of luck and being at the right place at the right time. But certainly not because I knew what I wanted when I got out of school and just went after it. I was just floating around. I thought I was going to have children and quit work, but things didn't work out that way.

Another woman told a similar story. In her case, however, college work experience landed her a job in the same city where her husband had accepted a graduate fellowship.

> I turned twenty-two the twentieth of May, I graduated from college on the third of June, and I got married on the tenth of June 1972. My husband had just graduated from a joint J.D.–M.B.A. program and received a fellowship to go to England. . . . So we went to London. I had worked for the First National Bank of Boston in Boston for two summers during college, and they were setting up a personal credit department in operations in London at the time that we were going to be there. . . . So they got me working papers, and I worked at the First National Bank of Boston in London basically as an assistant in different departments. . . . Before going, my husband interviewed at places in Boston, Philadelphia, and New York. He took a job in Boston, so we knew that we were coming back there. When we got back, I took a job with a consulting group as a research assistant.

Others made investments as wives and future mothers by supporting their husbands through graduate school. One woman described why she took her first job:

> Immediately after I graduated from college, I took a job as a bank teller, primarily because I was engaged at the time to my husband. He was not working, and I thought it would be a good idea to get a job right away and start generating income. I was qualified to teach but my teaching position fell through, so I just took the first job that was available. His parents paid his tuition to law school, but I paid for everything else.

Thus, although the majority of these women were not thinking in terms of careers or career goals, they were gaining work experience and skills as they followed their husbands' progress. In hindsight, one woman concluded, "All the jobs that I had contributed to a knowledge and a background that have been very helpful to me." These women found that they enjoyed working outside the home and began to develop confidence in themselves both as workers and as competitors within the organizational stratum they occupied as secretaries, administrative assistants, and other lower-level white-collar workers.

Although most of the women described their transition from job to career as a breakthrough of sorts, most also experienced it as a slow process of revelation in which several factors were important. Some were inspired, both positively and negatively, by their husbands. One husband encouraged his wife to start her career and then to cement it with an advanced degree. She recalled:

> I was obviously very bored with myself, and it was showing up in the relationship. I didn't know what to do with myself when the job ended at five o'clock. I was bored with it. And I was depending on Don for attention and depending a lot on him to entertain me. . . . He really pushed me to go back to school to get an M.B.A., out of a sense of how frustrated and bored I was.

Her husband concurred: "She was making me crazy by depending on me too much. I tried to push her to really go after opportunities." Another husband revealed that his encouragement was not based on any long-range plan—quite the contrary:

> I don't know why I encouraged her at the time. I don't know if I thought I would gain anything by her going back to school. There was no rational reason or long-term future plan for us. It just drove me crazy that Natalie had a lot of potential, and she wasn't pursuing it with a master plan.

In contrast, another woman, now a project editor at a consulting firm, left a flexible but low-paying position as a college lecturer in reaction to the traditional female role of financial dependency:

> I have never liked being dependent on somebody for my daily needs. I'm much more comfortable supporting than being supported—much more comfortable. And I think, from that point of view, the paycheck matters. I wasn't paid very much when I was teaching, and this makes a difference.

Thus, the shift from a job to a career could come about through a spouse's support or as a negative reaction to a traditional role.[3]

Women who started their careers after marriage commonly cited a combination of husbands' encouragement, security in marriage, and a new perception of their own situation.[4] One woman's initial unwillingness to recognize her capabilities was overcome, in part, with her husband's help:

> My husband married somebody very different from the person I am today. He likes me better now than he liked me then. He could see the potential [laughs]. It has to do with this feeling of self-confidence. You know, it's like when you get good grades, and you say, "How did I fool all those people?" Maybe you've run into this before and maybe you haven't, but what I mean is, I would never

3. It is noteworthy that no women reported active opposition or discouragement from their husbands; the absence of spousal opposition to a partner's career is a defining characteristic of the dual-career marriage.

4. In a study of undergraduates, Matina Horner (1969) found that career achievement was perceived as a male domain. Horner argued that women, unlike men, have a motive for *avoiding* success, fearing that achievement will have disastrous consequences for their identity as women. Despite the controversy surrounding Horner's findings, it is perhaps not surprising, then, that the majority of the women I interviewed "discovered" their aspirations and built self-confidence within the context of marriage, where their female identity would be less threatened.

> accept the fact that I was as good as I was. . . . At some point you start to believe that you're good and that you're capable and that you have a right to feel the way you do and a right to your own opinions. . . . It makes you feel more confident in your work; it makes you realize that you do have a career, not just a job—that you are building toward something and that you'll continue to.

The new self-perception and self-confidence this woman portrays combines her husband's positive appraisal with a realization, developed from interacting with co-workers, that she was, indeed, "good." For other women, positive comparisons with other career women and (particularly) men shift their attention away from bio-social definitions toward an assessment based on new criteria. One woman who dropped out of college returned to get a business degree because she saw that the skills of her male co-workers were more highly valued in building a career than was relying on personality alone.

> I realized that I had a lot of motivation. I really had a lot of interest in business. . . . I decided I needed more schooling, and I had to have definable skills. . . . I hate having to peddle myself, and I wanted to have something that would make them think, "Hey, this is valuable." I even wanted something male-oriented, and I knew at the time that business was still kind of a male profession. [Why male-oriented?] So that I would be treated seriously as a peer rather than as some sort of object. . . . I just didn't want to have to depend on my personality for a career.

Another woman recalled, "After a year with that corporation, I decided that I was as smart as any of those guys, and I was earning one-third of what they were earning. I said to my husband, 'Well, I'm going to business school.' "

As women's perceptions of their situations change,

the separate yardsticks against which a "successful" male and a "successful" female are measured can also shift. Instead of two independent yardsticks to judge the man as provider and the woman as homemaker and mother, one yardstick may evolve in which the masculine prototype prevails. Worth is measured for both men and women in terms of career status and the size of the paycheck. One woman, who initially had a traditional "feminine" career as a social worker, cited both her work with lawyers, who knew she was as smart as they were (although paid less), and the following story about "feminine worth" as the factors that convinced her to go back to school for a business degree.

> We'd go to parties, and everybody would talk to Bob because he was a lawyer. I was just sort of out on the side trying to start a conversation and talk about what I did, because that was real ego to me. I wanted to be a good mother, but then I didn't get any ego boost out of being a good mother, either. . . . I was tired of thinking I was as smart as my husband. . . . I wanted a paycheck equal to Bob's, and I wanted to have the career that I could talk about, that I was proud of, and that people would talk to me about. Indeed, that happened when I went to get an M.B.A. It's probably more a function of my being proud of it and liking what I'm doing than a function of the people that I talk to changing that much.

For the one-third of the women who married in their mid- to late twenties, working was assumed to be part of their marital relationship. Although their lives did not require them to follow their husbands from one position to the next, career beginnings for half of this group were also incremental. Regardless of which route they took to their careers—by following husbands from one job to the next or from career beginnings that preceded marriage—women's career decisions became intertwined with their husbands'.

In any case, once these women began to consider themselves career-oriented, they sought to acquire the additional training or certification necessary to enhance their chances of promotion. Table 6 shows that fully 71 percent of all women interviewed had earned a postgraduate degree in a field related to their work. The percentage of women who earned postgraduate degrees is the same for those married before and after they began their careers.

Equally important, once careers were started, the wife's earnings became a significant contribution to the couple's shared lifestyle. They did not just live on his salary, banking hers. Instead, they lived on both incomes and their lifestyle changed accordingly—including their rent or mortgage, their bills, the places they chose to go, and so forth. They became dependent on their dual earnings. As husbands and wives individually told me over and over, "We could live on one salary. We could adjust. But we

TABLE 6. Marriage and Advanced Education for Women

| *Postgraduate Degree* | *Married Before Career Began* N = 14 | *Married After Career Began* N = 7 |
|---|---|---|
| M.B.A. | 6 | 2 |
| M.A. (other nonbusiness) | 2 | 1 |
| J.D. | 2 | 1 |
| M.D. | 0 | 1 |
| Total | 10/14 | 5/7 |

NOTE: All the women in the sample had B.A.s.

couldn't live the same way we live today on two salaries." In other words, their joint earnings determine their standard of living, while at the same time their standard of living determines how much money they need to earn. Without necessarily planning to do so, these women have come to accrue financial obligations and debts and are experiencing the same kind of career pressure as men.

At the time the interviews were conducted, the women in this study occupied fairly diverse management or management-level positions in the Chicago business community. Table 7 lists in broad terms the positions they held.

TABLE 7. Organizational Positions and Activities of Dual-Career Wives

| *Position/Title* | *Number* | *Associated Activities* |
|---|---|---|
| Vice-president | 5 | International business<br>Planning |
| Director | 2 | Public relations<br>Personnel |
| Manager | 9 | Advertising and marketing<br>Tax accounting<br>Communications<br>Special projects |
| Professional | 3 | Corporate law<br>Medicine (doctor/professor)<br>Corporate accounting |
| Consultant | 2 | Marketing<br>Strategic planning |
| Total | 21 | |

Each of these women foresaw a reasonable probability of promotion; none saw herself locked into her present position. However, some did foresee corporate moves (within Chicago) as critical for their career advancement. Their dreams of career success today match those of their husbands and their male colleagues.

## THEIR CAREER: MARRIAGE

As described at the beginning of this chapter, work shapes the marriage. Yet, because *both* husbands and wives work—and, more important, have careers with similar and competing demands for commitment—a marriage can no longer respond entirely to the demands of only one spouse or spouse's career. Marriage can no longer serve to define a division of labor between breadwinner and homemaker or, with that division of labor, the relative priority or valuation of the different activities. If two careers are to be nourished, they must also be constrained by a set of rules about how competing demands are to be compromised and how the homemaking or reproductive activities of the marriage are to be organized. Among the couples I interviewed, the predominant mechanism for negotiating individual careers is based on marriage as a third career. For these couples, marriage meant both the social contract entered into by a man and a woman for intimacy, love, children, and all the intangibles of such a union as well as the conjoining of two careers. Thus, marriage comes to represent the subordination of two individual careers to a shared career development that has a variable influence counter to that of the organizations that structure formal economic careers.

This conception of a shared career infuses these marriages with a meaning different from that of traditional marriages. Although couples do not always articulate clear statements about the equity of careers and the equality of spouses, the practice of balancing the demands of two careers requires that some concept of mutual benefit be employed daily if both careers are to survive, rather than one atrophying into a job through a refusal to meet the employer's requirements for career mobility. This criterion of mutual benefit aids in distributing or accomplishing reproductive and homemaking choices and is used as a guide when either spouse confronts a situation that challenges or potentially affects the status of the other spouse's career. The approach couples take in resolving career conflicts is a product of an incremental process of decision making informed by a belief in and commitment to a shared third career—the marriage.

## *Equity, Symmetry, and Conflict*

Whereas marriage does partially shape the individual careers of spouses, careers have relatively more effect in altering the traditional roles of husband and wife. Gender roles continue to play a part in determining the form of marital relations, and dual-career couples face a constant struggle not to fall back on the old rules and roles of marriage that they witnessed as children. Marital equity is not taken for granted; it is worked for. As one husband said, "I certainly don't think this is a gloriously equal marriage marching off into the sunset. I think we struggle for equality all the time. And we remind each other when we are not getting it." For two careers to flourish simultaneously, equity in these marriages becomes crucial. But it is not an ideology of marital equality that determines careers; rather, equality becomes an issue *because* of the two careers. Indeed, couples rarely spoke directly about equality. They spoke instead of trying to strike a balance between careers and family commitments by keeping each other in check, so that neither spouse could tip the scale in favor of his or her own career. Although symmetry may produce feelings of equity, the attempt to maintain this symmetry provides a constant source of conflict within dual-career marriages. One man explains how this balancing act makes his marriage and career different from the traditional marriages of his colleagues:

> There is this constant pressure of trying to balance things, constantly reassessing how much time we spend in family and careers. [Could you give me an example?] Sure. Every day. Every week. Trying to figure out how much time to spend—whether I should be with the kids, or with Ann, or working. I know other men of my generation that basically work eighty hours a week on their careers, and their spouse is home in the kitchen and with the kids. Everything else is done by the spouse. And that is not possible in our household. The same goes for Ann. She competes in a world in which men also spend sixty or seventy hours a week working solely on their career, and they don't have other pressures because their spouses take care of all those things. That's not her world. She can't work all the time because she has other responsibilities. So you make definite trade-offs. You *both* make a trade-off. It's also hard because we both frequently talk about it—how much trade-off each one of us should be making, whether we are both making the same amount, or whether one of us feels that the other one is spending too much time on the job.

Similar tensions may arise in the traditional family, but the difference for dual-career couples is that the individual's trade-off of work and family is affected by the work demands of the other spouse. Children further complicate the picture. This husband revealed what he sees as the critical ingredient to achieving parity:

> When I feel I am getting away from how I would like my life to be, I try to make adjustments to what I do, or I may say, "You've got to come home," or "You've got to stay late," or "I can't come home early every day this week." You have to make that kind of blunt adjustment. If one of us thinks the other one is not doing what they should be doing overall, he has to come out and say it. She's got to tell me as well.

Although couples do not keep ledgers to measure equity on a regular basis, most couples have instituted rules about job choices and moves. After a heated argument in which they sought their parents' opinions about a husband's job offer in another city, one couple decided to establish a rule to prevent disagreements over job moves from recurring. The wife explained why she felt this a priori rule reflected their sense of marital equity:

> What we have tried to do is set the ground rules before we are faced with a specific decision. [Why?] To give it some neutrality. So that we weren't setting the ground rules in terms of what one person wanted to do or didn't want to do. We were setting the ground rules that could affect either of us equally, and then when the situation came up, we had a decision structure.

They decided that "whoever did not have the offer made the basic decision to move. If he had an offer, I had first crack at rejecting the city. It's really a veto power." Other couples had different mechanisms for achieving parity, including rules about lateral moves as well as promotions.

In another important aspect of negotiation, couples evaluate one partner's career and professional strengths against the other's. This practice offers a way of making decisions, but it can also be a source of conflict. One woman explained how she worked out this problem within the marriage:

> We always felt ourselves to be equal in our relationship. Certainly intellectual equals. Any problem I've ever had in that regard was me. . . . I spent three years dating my husband as he went through the joint J.D.–M.B.A. program, listening to all his friends talk about marketing as a bunch of bullshit. . . . I got to Harvard Business School and I really excelled in marketing. . . . I tended to say, "Oh, yeah, but that's just marketing." I went through a stage where I didn't think I could do anything better than he could. That really bothered me. I was having trouble with the relationship until I began to accept that there were things I was better at, things that I could bring to the relationship.

But marital symmetry can also be affected by how each individual feels about his or her own career. Disparate work experiences may lead to a temporary imbalance within the marriage. One wife explained how this power balance has alternated between her and her husband:

> For us the worst times are when one of us is doing particularly well and one of us is doing particularly badly—having problems at work and, as a result, feeling threatened. Then the power relationship at home starts developing, and the person who is feeling threatened starts feeling powerless.
>
> It was hard for Don when he was depending on me for financial support until his company became stable. It was hard for me when my situation in my present job had deteriorated badly and the whole thing felt shaky just when he was having this great success. . . . When we are both on a relatively even keel, not having disparate experiences, the relationship works best for us and just removes the power thing as an issue.

The marriage thus comes to operate as a constraint on the unbridled pursuit of one career to the possible disadvantage of the other. But it also operates as a buffer, cushioning the negative impacts of failures or reversals in one or the other career. The unpredictability of careers demands such an arrangement, and, paradoxically, it creates an emphasis on equity and symmetry for each career. Were it not for the fact that marriage is elevated in importance so that it can constrain as well as buffer, then one might refer to the relationship merely as a convenience. But because the marital tie is viewed as equal in importance to (if not more important than) the separate careers, it can operate as a legitimate constraint on those careers. The demands of two careers not only cause tension between two economic actors, but they also stimulate a review of traditional marital roles. It is the practice of combining two careers, not the articulation of a nonsexist ideology, which shapes decisions and informs change.

### *Taking a Step Out of Traditional Gender Roles*

I was a product of a family where the mother didn't ever work and whose job, in her mind, and whose responsibility in that marriage was the maintenance of the household, the parenting function, cooking meals, and keeping things organized, so that when my dad got home, he didn't have to put up with anything. . . . Joan [the speaker's wife] says, "I'm not going to scurry around here at ten minutes to six and clean up the house so it looks neat and clean when you get home so you can think that's the way it's been all day. You can help clean it up." But that was not the way my mother was. I guess I wouldn't have as honest a view of the world and life and I wouldn't enjoy it as much if someone with a broom was dusting a path in front of me as I walked.

Firsthand knowledge of the organization of family life comes from what we observed our parents doing. Outsiders are rarely privy to the social organization of life in families other than their own. Therefore, even if couples have friends in dual-career marriages, they are more likely to compare themselves to their parents, rather than to their friends. Like the husband quoted above, the majority of individuals in this study came from families that had clearly defined roles and expectations for husbands and wives. But just as this man's father did not have a firsthand understanding of what it took to run his home, neither did his wife fully comprehend the work he did. Furthermore, he was the "king of the castle" and derived his status from his role as breadwinner.

Although the point of my interviews was not to investigate the link between these couples' experiences and those of their parents, I did ask about parents' occupations and economic standing in an effort to determine whether dual-career couples had prior exposure to or encouragement for their current lifestyles. The interviews revealed that between 60 and 70 percent of the respondents came from what can be regarded as working- or middle-class backgrounds. Self-reported assessments of their parents' class positions described 71 percent of these individuals as coming from the working class or the middle class. A more objective assessment, based on their fathers' occupations, netted a somewhat different distribution: roughly 60 percent had either working- or middle-class backgrounds; the remainder came from upper-middle-class or upper-class families. Fathers' occupations among the former group included presser in a clothing factory, subway motorman, civil servant, grocery clerk, regional sales manager for a utility company, and small-business owner. Among the latter group, only two respondents' fathers held positions as corporate executives; the rest either were independent professionals (such as accountants, lawyers, or doctors) or were owners of large businesses. The overwhelming majority of the respondents' mothers did not work outside the home. Only five of the forty-two interviewees reported that their mothers worked outside the home; of those five only one mother worked full-time or began working once her children were teenagers. Thus, these dual-career couples did not have a parental example to emulate.

Yet, things changed for these couples. There was no ideological underpinning to their marriages that caused the roles of husband and wife to be dramatically altered. Rather, the upheaval and break with their traditional upbringing had a simple explanation: as women's careers became as demanding as their husbands', there was no time for a wife to be a traditional homemaker. The initial change, then, occurred in the wife's role. Asked to comment on the difference between male and female expectations about paid work, one woman said:

> I made a choice to work, and I like it. And I do it because I like it. I mean, I wasn't socialized to think I was a bad person if I didn't work, when most men never really had that choice. They've always known they were going to work. They were going to support a family, and they never were able to make a choice. But I did. It's very important to me, or I wouldn't have made the choice.

Although this may sound like a personal and idiosyncratic choice, it is in fact a gender role decision. Implicit in the choice to work outside the home is not only a comparison with men's roles but also a confrontation between traditional values and new desires. Even though most women describe their careers as products of a choice, the choice to pursue a career also constitutes a decision *not* to pursue a traditional role as homemaker.

On the other side, one of the men I interviewed credited his wife's and his own ability to change as the keys to his present outlook:

> A lot of people put their spouses in fixed roles. I don't do that. If my wife wanted to do something else in the future—something new, something different—great. A lot of people can't handle changes—rapid changes. I roll with the punches. You know, it's better to swim with the current than to swim against it. So, my views on some things—maybe you'd call them enlightened—really exist because of my relationship with my wife.

Although women's roles have changed, another man felt that women's expectations of men as breadwinners had remained constant.

> As far as I'm concerned, her career is all add-on, additional, extra, because it's more than I expected out of marriage. [What do you mean?] The money, the bright, intelligent woman who's active and involved—that kind of thing. That's much more than I expected, whereas I don't think I'm that much more than she was raised to expect. She knew since the time she was a kid she was going to marry a professional—somebody to provide well for her. Whereas I was raised with the notion that I would be the breadwinner and the wife would be the cook and mother and housekeeper.

In a way, he is not wrong; neither husbands nor wives are looking for role reversal. However, as wives and husbands become "duplicates" of one another (at least as workers outside the home), her new role does alter his. The invisible work of the home is now in plain view, and although couples do hire household labor, many chores remain to be done. One husband explained how this change came about for him and his wife: "We don't consciously say that we're going to share, but it just turns out, with both people working, you can't have one person do everything. If one of us were relying on the other to fix meals, we'd both starve."

The wife's career not only alters the meaning of "wife" but also, in the process, alters the man's role as "husband." This role expansion is fundamentally different for men and women: she has moved outward to discover the world of making a living, and he has moved inward to discover the intricacies of running a home. This is not to suggest that individuals do not have lingering ambivalences connected with giving up clearly defined husband-wife patterns, nor am I implying that couples have completely shed traditional roles. The reality is much more complicated.

The social organization of dual-career family life creates the appearance that husbands' and wives' roles are somewhat interchangeable. Yet, their feelings toward their roles may shed a different light on the picture. Ambivalence in their struggle away from traditional gender role patterns may stem from stereotypical views of masculine-feminine differences for some and from guilt about not fulfilling traditional gender roles for others. One husband explained the origins of a gender-based division of labor in his home in this way:

> You have to realize I was in the 4-H Club with the cows, and my wife was in the 4-H Club with home economics. That tells a lot about where we started. But we have migrated away from that. . . . Even today my wife is not embarrassed by doing squaw work. She kind of likes to do it. It gives us an old-fashioned feeling to our marriage every once in a while, and that is a nice touch.

Some women worry about emasculating their husbands by asking them to do more around the house, even if they employ full-time housekeepers. One woman related how her feelings about masculinity and femininity stand in the way of pushing her husband to do more:

> This is hard for me to describe, but Mike's conception of himself is fairly macho. . . . I can't just destroy his ego and still have a good relationship. Much of him is defined by his blood brothers, who he hangs around with. They are married to women who stay at home. . . . I don't want to make him feel like some sort of freak. I have a real fear of making him feel this way. I don't know if it's justified or not, but I know that it would be far from the norm if I said to him, "From now on you're doing 50 percent of the laundry, you're fixing dinner every other night. You're doing this. You're doing that." I would feel very much like I was just demoralizing him.

It is unclear whether this woman fears emasculating her husband or whether she fears the ramifications for her and for their relationship of giving up those traditional chores that represent femininity. Other women do worry more directly about "losing their femininity," which, at least from this data, appears to be embodied in the chores performed by the traditional wife. One woman, explaining why she insists on doing one particular chore herself despite her husband's insistence otherwise, said, "I don't like the way he looks doing the laundry. Well, to me it's something that women do. It represents a nurturing activity to me—something very feminine. Maybe it's my way of showing him I still have that." Other women wonder how their husbands' careers might be affected because, unlike other corporate wives, they are not helping him climb the corporate ladder. Speaking of business social events, one woman expressed the "what if" concern:

> I am definitely odd because I have a career, and I think it may have possibly done damage to Al. . . . It's a partnership organization, and if I had been sort of a traditional, suburban wife at home, we conceivably could have gotten into the act of entertaining the others in order to be social rather than professional figures to them, which would have been to his advantage.

Her husband did know about this worry of hers, but he had diminished the importance of socializing, whereas she continued to think about it.

Another woman, although not typical of the group, presented a different twist in how she and her husband hold on to a piece of the traditional:

> We have quite a size differential. I'm just over five feet; Dan is six feet tall, outweighs me by about eighty-five pounds, is physically powerful, and can physically do things I can't do. . . . That has allowed us to maintain something of the traditional roles without having to do any traditional role playing.

The majority of women retain a certain traditionalism in response to their own ambivalence about new gender roles. But the men are much more likely to see women's gender role expansion as a loss of the kind of time and attention traditional wives once gave husbands, especially when there are children. One man described his wife's career as an "extra dimension" that had attracted him to her in the first place. Yet, this source of attraction was simultaneously a source of conflict. Below he explains why:

> We went through a little marriage counseling back in the early days of our marriage, which I guess really saved our marriage. This wise old goat said, "You know, oftentimes people marry for the same exact reasons that split up the marriage." You marry somebody because they are working

and "with it," and then you get married and things turn around a little bit because they are busy. You don't get their full attention, and you feel like you are being slighted, and that drives a wedge into the whole marriage. This happens sometimes with us. But we are more partners than in the traditional family, where there is a male breadwinner and a woman who is the housekeeper and mother. My wife's working and her having that extra dimension adds that dimension to our relationship and our marriage.

It is in the emotional arena, perhaps, that men feel most slighted. The attention wives once showered on their husbands is reduced because the women no longer have the time, or energy, or perhaps even the need to show it. One man talked about the way he sometimes feels:

But I have a few misgivings. Sometimes I think it would be better for me if she didn't work, in that the time she spends with the baby in the evenings would be devoted to me. She would need more adult companionship then. You know, she comes home beat up from business like everybody else. She doesn't need an adult to talk to. If she was with the two-year-old all day long, she'd have to be bonkers at the end of the day and need adult company. But I know the way I feel in this respect is selfish.

Another man described how he felt when his wife first began to work full-time:

At first it caused a lot of pain, and there were times that I felt quite misused. Because when she first took on full-time work, she was almost not my wife. She really did separate psychologically, physically, and every other way. She just was so involved in getting started in this job that I was left with almost everything, including the chores.

Similar feelings were expressed by another man about his wife working evenings:

> Right now, my wife is in a very busy time, so she brings work home every night. . . . That's why I sometimes bring my work home, because it gives me something to do when she works. We spend less time with each other because she's working, and it bothers me. I understand that she does it because she has to, because she has a responsibility to people, but I don't necessarily like it.

Although men are involved in the domestic arena, their feelings are not necessarily aligned with their actions, and, to some extent, this calls into question gender role definitions. As one man put it:

> You know, I don't consider myself the ultimate liberated man. In terms of the pendulum swing, I'm pretty far in that direction [left]. But you know, when she's had to work on Saturdays or Sundays to finish a big project, I take care of the kids and I'm not overly thrilled about it. But I do it.

The majority of men earn as much as or more than their wives, and thus the sense of masculinity they derive from their role as a provider (even though they are no longer the sole provider) is less likely to be threatened.[5] One man, however, did think about this:

> In a traditional marriage, a wife normally has to deal with the demands of running the home and the husband has to deal with the demands of a job. In a dual-career marriage, those spheres overlap almost to the extent of becoming one. . . . I don't feel competitive with my wife, but that's qualified to the extent that if she were making $100,000 a year and I were making $30,000, I can't say that I would not in that circumstance feel differently. . . . There were periods in our marriage where she made $3,000 more than

5. Model (1982) found that higher-income men in dual-career families contribute more to household work if they are married to women with comparable incomes. The greater the difference between husbands' and wives' incomes, the less involved husbands are in parenting and other domestic responsibilities.

> I did, and it didn't bother me because essentially, as I view it, we are exactly even. I think in that circumstance it's rather difficult to feel like a lace is untied. If she earned significantly more, it just might come untied.

Husbands and wives both are concerned about how their new roles might affect their children—another example of how shifting gender roles are called into question. The "success" or "failure" of raising their children will only be clear to them a decade or more hence, but for the time being, this question gnaws at them.

### *Career Development and Choice*

Even though the steps out of traditional gender roles are somewhat tentative and cause some discomfort, the conjoining of two careers does open some real possibilities for change in careers and work relationships. In most cases the development of careers follows an alternating pattern. The husband's career comes first and makes possible the wife's career or investments leading to it. Her career then allows shifts in his career. Perhaps more important than the alternating character of career investments is that the large and stable portion of family income generated by the wife's career makes alternative career options possible for the man. For example, the dual-career marriage frees men from sole economic responsibility. Men can be less obsessed by work, less aggressive, and even less motivated because the weight of this responsibility is shared. This shift has made a difference in this man's life:

> My business acquaintances and friends make easily four times what I make. They really bust their humps. They are out traveling and working long nights and weekends. One

> of the questions I've always had is, would I really want to do that anyway? But I can stay at the low end of that category and be less aggressive, but still be in that category, because my wife works.

Another man considered what he'd gained by not having to be a workaholic:

> I'm not a workaholic. I'm pretty comfortable with what I'm doing. I probably could make more money if I was interested in working a lot harder, but I would have to sacrifice a lot of things for that—like time with my family, personal time, a lot of things. I'm just not willing to do that, and in part, I don't have to do that because my wife works.

It is not clear from this data whether individual careers suffered or did not progress as quickly because of the dual-career marriage. Although career decisions may be constrained for one individual at a particular point in time, at other times this marriage may provide a cushion that expands opportunities for the individual. This is particularly true for the men in this study. When mid-life crisis occurred and the wife's salary was substantial (with, perhaps, savings in the bank), several men did not just fantasize about a career change, but they acted on the desire, and their wives encouraged such moves. For several other men, a career shift was in the talking stages. Thus, the dual-career marriage can pave the way for career choice.[6] After having a disagreement with the president of the company he worked for, one man, who had

6. Gilbert (1985, 35–36), who studied only men in dual-career marriages, found that 54 percent of the husbands reported that their marriage had some effect on their work goals. Nearly half of this group felt "less pressure to provide for the family economically and more freedom to explore other career options and to risk career changes." However, the other half of this group believed that their wives' careers limited opportunities for husbands' career development in several ways: fewer hours were available for their work; men sometimes had to settle for a job that was not their first choice; or they sometimes had to alter their level of aspiration.

wanted to "strike out on his own" in the consulting field, did just that. He explains how this was possible:

> We [with a partner] went into business with virtually no clients. The fact that Susan was working and making a good income was significant. The decision would have been different if that had not been the case. We couldn't have afforded it. She and I talked about my leaving the company, and she agreed with me. She didn't like the consulting thing, but the idea of me being on my own also appealed to her.

However, the business did not quickly gain a solid footing, and after a period of time this started to affect their marriage:

> It's good we started to make money when we did. It took a bit longer than we expected. We'd both reached a point where if we hadn't started being more successful within a year, I probably would have gone back into the job market. If I hadn't, she would have been pretty unhappy about it. She was feeling the pressure of carrying the financial responsibility and feeling that the sacrifice we were making collectively was beginning to add up.

Shared economic responsibility is the goal of these couples, and in this particular case the wife learned that being the primary support was not what she wanted. Men have always had to contend with the pressure to work. This wife learned firsthand how this pressure felt, and it placed a wedge in their marriage, which disappeared once his business began to make money.

In another case the wife had more interest in pursuing a corporate career than her husband did. He was a successful vice-president in a major insurance company, and he wanted out. Approaching his mid-forties, he married a woman almost ten years younger (a second marriage for both), and like a runner in a relay race, he passed the career baton to her. The wife described why he made the decision to leave the corporate game and to take a job with a nonprofit organization:

> It was very much a mutual decision. Louis hated the rat race, as he used to call it. Not that he wouldn't have done it, but he was past the point of really enjoying it. He didn't enjoy going to work every day. I was still very interested in my career. So we looked at the decision objectively.

He explained how this decision was possible:

> We made a decision. I thought her career had a lot more potential than my career. . . . I didn't want to work late anymore, and I didn't want to travel and stuff like that. I really think that's what it takes to really get ahead. I'm talking about big, big dollars and big, big jobs. I'm not willing to make that kind of commitment to a job, and Jean is, and I hope she makes it. . . . So her career has meant that I could do what I want to do. It's given me a lot of flexibility and the ability to be fairly free.

He currently is her chief adviser when it comes to organizational issues, but because they are in completely different fields the business expertise is hers.

One husband, who has an M.B.A. and an M.D., decided that in the next couple of years he wants to leave a research-administrative post to pursue his own practice. Although such a venture could conceivably be undertaken as a sole earner, the dual-career marriage facilitates career shifts.

> Now I find I'm more interested in clinical medicine. It's certainly a help to have some financial security—so if I decide to go into practice solely, it would not be a disaster for the family because she's earning. It is a major insurance policy. Similarly, if she didn't like her job, she could leave, because I offer her financial security.

This woman told of the freedom she feels she gives her husband because of their two-career marriage:

> The woman who works and makes as much as the man gives the man flexibility and freedom in his job. He doesn't have to worry incessantly: "What if something happens—what if I die or what if I get fired or what if I hate this career and I'd rather refinish furniture and start my own business?" He has more flexibility because of the economic freedom.

Another man talked of his job fantasies, knowing that his marriage just might offer him the freedom to realize them:

> My idea of a perfect job is to announce for a baseball team, and I'm perfectly serious. I love baseball. I could do that forever. . . . One of the things I've thought about is I would love to own an antique shop or a bookstore and just do that. . . . Sometimes I think I don't like being in the rat race. I don't want to have pressures, but to be able to do something I really enjoy that's relaxing. . . . I can seriously think about these things, not just fantasize, because there is always a fallback position—my wife's working. . . . The problem would be if both of us decided we wanted to rely on the other person. We couldn't do it. But that's not going to happen, partly because Cindy likes what she is doing and likes the business world and will continue to do it. I am more flexible in that I may want to do something else.

The dual-career marriage often offers husbands the freedom to explore career alternatives and career shifts. Women in this study have not yet explored this freedom, perhaps because their careers are newer (both in terms of defining their work as a career and in the number of years they have spent in their chosen fields). Eventually, some of these wives may find that their husbands' career changes will in turn allow alternatives in the women's work lives.

Among this new elite group of couples, men also derive prestige from having career wives. In the 1950s a homemaker wife was a symbol of a man's successful fulfillment of his role as a breadwinner. In the 1980s the emphasis is no longer on the man-as-breadwinner but rather on having each partner participate in providing financially. Vitality, personal growth, and being mutually interesting are now the important criteria by which these couples judge their success as spouses. For them, marriage can be a springboard for self-actualization. Husbands and wives alike agreed that self-esteem and self-fulfillment were as important for women as for men—perhaps even more so because these qualities help to make a spouse interesting. One husband defined fulfillment in this way:

> She wasn't being fulfilled with what she was doing. [What do you mean by fulfilled?] It means you become more centered and your energy becomes more focused. You are indeed happier. Your talents are being used often to their utmost. You are growing. . . . I think every mature adult needs more than the home as the center of your life in some all-encompassing way. At least I think Barb does, and I think that is the only way you stay interesting as a person.

I asked men what they thought would happen if their wives decided not to work. Besides citing the loss of income, which would affect their lifestyle (the issue behind my question), men believed that their wives' self-esteem would be affected and that they themselves would lose the status they indirectly derive from their wives' careers. As one man stated:

> Right now we are living on two salaries. If one of us quit work, we could not continue to live in the manner in which

> we currently live. . . . We've gotten used to living on two salaries. So, there is the purely financial aspect of it. I also like the fact that Lynda works. I must admit that I do feel a bit more "something" about our relationship than the people I work with who basically have stay-at-home wives. I can't explain what I mean by that something.

Another man expressed what that "something" meant to him:

> I think she has to work for ego satisfaction. I've said to her that if she doesn't work, that's fine with me. But it would be very tight if she stopped working. I'd have to pick up additional expenses, and she needs the satisfaction, I believe, that she gets out of working. I'm very proud of her because I think she is a really sharp business person, and she needs that for her own happiness. . . . She's very good at what she does. She gets a lot of ego gratification out of her work, plus it's a bit of an ego trip for me to have a wife who's so powerful. I like that. I like that kind of thing.

Similar feelings were expressed by this man, who described how having a wife with a career reflects differently on men than does having a wife with a job:

> I was talking to a physician, and he asked me why I arrived at the hospital so early. I said, "Well, my wife works, and I have to get back to relieve the sitter." The look on his face when I said my wife works said, "Geez, Mark's practice must be terrible, his wife is working." Then my colleague said, "Oh, what does she do?" expecting me to say she types manuscripts. Well, I said, "She's an economist with X corporation, and she does corporate planning." Well, his eyes then changed as if to see me in a new light.

A new source of self-fulfillment and self-esteem for women is provided not through domestic work but rather through participation in the labor force. Paid work is central to many women's self-esteem because it provides them with an independent identity. One woman contrasted the meaning of work for her to her husband's view:

> He's a person that needs a career as a means of making money, so that he can indulge himself. . . . I'm much more a person whose career is of primary importance. It's not just a means to an end. I get satisfaction if I do a good job and I'm promoted. I'd go crazy at home. I could never, never stay at home. Work is a fundamental part of my identity and something very separate from my husband.

Another woman put it simply: "It gives me a sense of being worth something."

Husbands and wives may measure their worth by how much money they earn. However, the self-esteem acquired through careers is reflected in the couples' perceptions about career marriages. An independent identity provides the basis for a greater measure of marital equality, as neither spouse is economically dependent on the other. This husband explained the meaning of his wife's career to their marriage:

> She has a sense of a full partnership and she should. . . . I think the partnership would be less equal if she didn't work, because she would sense herself as being far less equal if she were not working and having that self-esteem.

No longer dependent, one woman captured the "new" meaning of marriage:

> Working has increased my status in terms of equality within the marriage, and it also has decreased my dependence, both my own sense of dependence and my husband's sense that I am somewhat dependent on him. That makes it into much more of a voluntary relationship than an involuntary one of my staying with him because I need to stay with him. He's not staying with me because he's obligated to somehow, and it just makes it into a much clearer situation. I'm

> here because I want to be here, not because I need to be here or because he feels trapped.

Since husbands and wives are no longer dependent on each other in the traditional sense, they must bring something to their marriage, almost daily, if it is to continue. The life they create that is external to the marriage (namely, their career experiences) is one of the fundamental ways these couples keep interested themselves, remain interesting to their partners, and help their marriages thrive. One man insisted his wife go back to her career because

> I think it's important for her to have a life of her own—something that she does, where she's a viable person, where she deals with people that are heads of companies, earns a relatively good dollar, and has her own life. She doesn't live off me. And I don't live off her. It's important to me that she does something very interesting, so that she is a growing person. I find her more interesting because she's working.

By remaining interesting individuals, these spouses help keep their marriages from turning stale; as this woman expressed it:

> I think there's a lot less friction in our lives. We're not just exhausted with each other. We're both busy with other things, and we bring a lot of different things to our relationship—different experiences that are similar in a lot of ways because we understand each other well.

### *Communication and Support*

Despite moments of doubt, ambivalence, and conflict, dual-career couples often develop a style of communication different from that found in traditional marriages. Husbands and wives with careers spend most of their time engaged in similar activities, which, though often involving different expertise, share a rhythm and a structure, unlike the chasm that separates paid employment and housework. Thus, I found these couples to have a different level of understanding about each other's lives, a level that is intimate and empathic. One husband described what this meant to him:

> She has a fundamental understanding of what it's like to be employed in the same fashion and manner that I am, and that gives her a capacity for not a specific understanding but a general understanding. Whereas I think that might be more difficult for a woman who had a lesser job or no job at all. It means I don't have to put up with criticism or harassment about working late or inattention to detail. She can forgive my forgetting a daily phone call. She can understand working late or she can understand the necessity of drinking after work with the people I work with or clients, I think, much more readily than she would if she were not employed in similar circumstances. She can understand being in a lousy mood when I come home and I am just crabby. . . . And I understand the demands of her job likewise.

Another man put it this way: "She has a sense of what I'm doing because she's out there doing the same damn thing every day."

Talking about the day's events over dinner or in bed is not unusual for most couples, regardless of whether there is one wage earner or two. But what is striking for two-career couples is the similarity of the partners' talk. She talks finance and he talks marketing. It is the content of her end of the conversation that has changed, as is apparent in this comment:

> I might tell her how I feel about something if she asks, but I don't know much about loans or the viability of the business or the people she's dealing with or her interest rate at

> specific times. I might use her as a sounding board for my work as well, but neither of us depends upon the other in terms of business decisions.

Another woman described a similar exchange in her marriage:

> We spend a portion of every day talking about work. You know, something particularly out of the ordinary that he happens to be doing—some unusual type of financing—or I'm running into a specific kind of problem and think it's unusual; we'll talk about that.

These couples can provide support for each other because they share similar work and organizational experiences. However, they are not conduits linking one firm to the next. Most talk primarily about personal problems, office politics, and unusual events that occurred during the day. Unless couples are in the same field, they do not talk about the details of work because specialized knowledge is required to understand the finer points of their jobs. Even when both are in the same field, they do not necessarily discuss specifics, especially when issues are confidential. One couple, consultants who work for competing firms, edits out any work-related topics from their conversation. The similarity of their employers' organizational structure, however, provides a rhythm for shared understanding and communication.

> We tend to stay out of the substance of what we are doing, which is where we can get into problems of confidentiality. . . . We talk a lot about common problems, like relating to the other associates. Her study teams are like my study teams. Her problems of having a junior associate who doesn't seem to be able to get his or her game together are the same as my problems, and we are a resource for each other in saying, "Have you tried this or that?" or "If you said that, here is how they could have reacted." A lot of

> times we have very useful conversations; sometimes we get on each other's nerves, but most of the time it's very useful. We talk about people that each of us knows, and we talk about office politics back and forth.

They offer each other advice and counsel about career decisions, occupational stumbling blocks, and personnel matters, such as how to handle a boss or how much of a pay raise to ask for. In some marriages one spouse may rely on the other for advice more often, as this woman explained: "I'm more the type of person who asks people for opinions about things. I think he is more confident about dealing with people than I am, and that has something to do with my asking for advice."

A few couples say they do share their expertise with each other. One woman, who is a management consultant, asks her lawyer husband for the legal help she needs for her work: "I would ask him, 'What do you think about this?' or if I had to read a legal document I'd certainly say, 'Please translate this.' I can't read that shit. So I'll ask him." This woman's husband asks her for less advice, because he tends to deal with legal issues that she knows nothing about. But other spouses may rely on each other for the information they need to get their jobs done.

> Sometimes we call each other up on the phone. For example, if he's dealing with some law firm that does bond work, he'll call me up and ask me if I can find out if the firm is good or has done stuff before. Sometimes I'll call him up for a mortgage schedule.

Of course, all couples talk to each other about topics not related to their careers—family, children, purchases, redecorating homes, vacations, and so on. But how does their talk of work contribute to their marriage? This different kind of communication has advantages and disadvantages. There is greater direct support for each other, as one man described:

> There's a bit of competition there, but not unhealthy. I read and critique things she's written, and I ask her to do the same. . . . I ask her for materials she may have that might be helpful, and I've given her materials that I think would be useful to her.

Another advantage is the greater potential for respect, stemming both from a spouse's ability to deliver an informed opinion as well as from greater understanding of each other.

> I listen to her, and I weigh her judgment. I make my decision, and sometimes it is very much in line with her ideas and sometimes it is not. What we discuss are business relationships: what am I going to say to person X in regard to a disagreement about something, or how am I going to handle the fact that I am angry about a decision? The same kinds of issues come up in Jill's business, so she understands.

Another husband recounted:

> We share ideas, that sort of thing. Barb is very much involved in what I am doing. We know what each other is doing in our day-to-day work, and we respect each other as far as business is concerned. She is a big help to me, and I think I'm a big help to her also. . . . She is much more a verbalizer when it comes to talking at home than I am. I tend to listen more.

A shared understanding of traveling can make a woman's relationship with her husband different from that of the traditional wife.

> Another aspect of my traveling and his traveling is that each of us understands what travel is to the other, and it's not sitting at home thinking that it's glamorous or exciting

> and that I'm being left out, as a lot of wives do who are very resentful of their husbands' traveling. We don't give each other hassles about traveling.

Yet, at the time of the interview, this woman felt badly that she was away so much:

> Al is up for consideration as principal in his firm, and it's a very difficult and trying time. I feel as if my travel has detracted from my ability to be a supportive person, because I've been away at a time when he has needed support and I haven't been able to give him as much as I would have been able to if I had been physically present.

Talking "work" also has the potential for creating competition for status between spouses. Sometimes couples commented that their talk led to disagreement about who knew best and who was really the expert. Many couples tended to resolve this problem by carving out distinct areas of expertise for each other.

> Our work coincidentally overlaps an awful lot, and we share a lot of the same professional interests. But we each have a reasonable working knowledge of where the other person is stronger. There's some recognition that I know more about certain things and she knows more about other things. . . . Sometimes we interrupt each other when we are talking about things, but if it is my area that I know more about, she backs off and vice versa.

This delineation of distinct areas of expertise or professional turf limits communication; but at the same time, it represents a way for couples to avoid getting too close to the worlds each spouse occupies outside the home. It is a way in which the marriage buffers the careers and helps husbands and wives from developing the petty jealousies and conflict characteristic of co-workers in the same office.

At the same time that communication provides valuable succor and insight for both husbands and wives, it can also go a long way toward reducing the stress that accompanies a corporate career. Many couples considered the first hour or so they spent together at the end of the work day as a time to "decompress." One man described the decompression period:

> I think both our employers have a couple of hardworking dumbbells . . . which puts a stress on our relationship here, because when we get home the first hour we don't talk, we scream. It is either scream or do an imitation of a mackerel by just flopping over.

Familiarity with the rigors of corporate work can supersede even patience as the most important part of the decompression process.

## CONCLUSION

At the outset of the chapter, I suggested that the dual-career couple represented a situation with "two husbands and no wife." However, this representation ignores synchronous developments in two other directions—partly toward limiting the career aspirations and goals of husbands and wives and partly toward opening new avenues of expression for both. This combination of new limitations and new opportunities offers fundamentally different arrangements from those of traditional marriages for couples who are willing to undertake the challenge of negotiating this terrain. Such negotiation includes not only two parties or acts of interest—his and hers—but also a third: "their" career, the marriage. Negotiations in these marriages shift back and forth, defining mutual interests in work and defining the relationship, which acts as a potential counterweight to the influence of work. This third "career" requires a clearer set of limits on the demands of the other careers, offering the possibility that marriage and family might exert some influence on what employers can ask of employees.

But, because dual-career marriages are few in number and because career couples tend to be employed in organizations that are capable of resisting collective demands from management staff, the influence of marriage on work tends to be reduced to selected incidents of individual resistance or, more commonly, opportunities foregone in order to sustain the balance between his career and hers. This situation makes it even more important to define a set of principles that can guide the pursuit of two careers and that can create an acceptable union between career and family. To this end, norms of equity and reciprocity must be much more widely discussed and debated. Because neither husband nor wife can claim sole authority on the basis of "breadwinning," rules of conduct and a division of labor must be created to service the equally compelling demands of two careers. But concerns with equity between husbands and wives rarely precede the dual-career marriage. Instead, such concerns commonly *follow* investments in two careers.

# 3

# MONEY MAKES A DIFFERENCE

MONEY DOES make a difference. Dual incomes enable these couples to spend far more on consumer items and to make major purchases earlier than one-income families. In 1981 the couples I interviewed enjoyed a median family income of $90,250. Median individual income was $40,500.[1] Both figures were far above the median family income for the United States, which at that time was $22,388 (U.S. Bureau of the Census, 1981). These couples own condominiums in the city or houses in the suburbs, and some own an additional weekend retreat or country home; other investments, such as stocks and bonds, tend to be minor and limited to a fraction of their total earnings. They generally do not worry about the price of furniture, clothing, or a night on the town. Most have achieved in their thirties a lifestyle of material luxury and comfort that others do not enjoy until much later in their lives, if ever. Although they could live on either spouse's income alone, all the couples in this study admitted that, to do so, they would have to give up major aspects of their present lifestyle. For many the loss of one income would mean a return to the controlled spending and stringent budgeting of their graduate school years.

1. Median income for the women was $40,200 (standard deviation of $18,806); for men the figure was $47,500 (standard deviation of $20,017).

Money makes a difference by liberating people from the conscious budgeting of family expenses. Large incomes allow immediate gratification of material desires, unobstructed by a budgeting mentality. Respondents were quick to tell me that they "do not budget money"—meaning that although they have fixed household expenses (mortgage payments, for example) their combined earnings are such that their purchasing power need not be consciously controlled or limited. They do not have to budget for a $500 dress or for the $3,000 airfare to rendezvous with a spouse on a consulting assignment abroad. They need not worry about earning money to live on day to day; instead, at this stage in their lives, they worry about where and how to profitably invest or shelter the surplus. In short, dual-career couples do not have the financial concerns of the majority of the U.S. population. Although these couples still want and feel they deserve more money for their work, acquiring basic material goods is no longer a primary objective.

Money has clearly enhanced the material well-being of these couples; but has it changed the relations between husbands and wives? Many feminists argue that cloistering women in the home has made it more of a prison than a shelter and has supported the unjust domination of husbands over wives (Friedan, 1963; Jones, 1970; Hartmann, 1981b; MacKinnon, 1981; Thorne, 1982; and Smith, 1975–1976). Has the participation of married women in the labor market actually diminished husbands' authority over wives? Much of the research about working wives has focused on women either as part-time workers or as partners in two-paycheck families. Those studies show that although working outside the home has increased some women's sense of self-worth, the mere fact that they hold jobs has not had fundamental effects on relations between husbands and wives. Women have not on the whole been freed from household chores but have instead added paid work to those duties.[2] Additionally, although working wives' income may be important, this contribution to family income does not substantially diminish the authority husbands exercise, particularly over financial affairs.

This lack of change in the division of household chores and in authority over major financial affairs can be largely attributed to the kinds of occupations most women have entered: the lower ranks of retail sales and nonprofessional or semi-skilled service work. These are primarily low-paying, low-status jobs that offer relatively little security and only meager opportunity for upward mobility. Simply having a job is not enough to alter traditional relations between husbands and wives. To exercise authority over financial decision making requires both the existence of discretionary income and the likelihood that that income will be relatively secure. Thus, a major distinction between dual-career families and lower- and middle-class families is that in the former case either spouse's income could support the family. For nearly every couple in this sample, the husband's or wife's earnings can (or in time could) support the family

2. Studies indicate that husbands of employed wives do more housework than husbands of nonemployed wives, although the employed women continue to be responsible for most of the housework. Among the most widely cited of such studies are those by Blood and Wolfe (1960), Nye and Hoffman (1963), Young and Willmott (1973), and Hoffman and Nye (1974). Time budgeting studies of working couples' daily activities report either no effect of a wife's employment on husband's housework time or at most a small positive effect (Walker, 1970; Meissner et al., 1975; Robinson et al., 1976; Berk and Berk, 1979). See Pleck (1977) for a critique of the latter studies. Studies of dual-career couples have found that couples are likely to hire help when the wife works, rather than having husbands assume more domestic tasks (Poloma and Garland, 1971; Safilios-Rothschild, 1970b; Gerstel and Gross, 1984).

unit. Moreover, these couples believe that their incomes are secure and that they will increase over time, which further distinguishes their financial position from that of other two-paycheck couples.

## MONEY AND AUTHORITY

Independent incomes can change the handling of financial affairs. Having two high and secure incomes increases the likelihood that couples will distinguish between individual and communal resources, thus allowing for greater equality in decision making about financial matters. However, most American families, let alone individual spouses, do not earn such incomes. Altering the usual pattern of pooling incomes (and resources) may only be possible because the couples in this study earn large sums of money; although they do not have to worry about having money, they do go to great lengths to devise systems for handling financial matters in their marriages. These couples appear to have different concerns about money entitlement (meaning how to spend their money and who should spend it) than do couples from other economic classes. However, large individual incomes are a necessary but not a sufficient condition for greater equality between husbands and wives in financial matters. Likewise, more egalitarian relationships in general in dual-career couples are possible but are not necessarily the case.

Probing the relationship between money and authority is difficult because money is a "sacred" topic and not easily discussed. Financial status is usually revealed indirectly by one's lifestyle, not directly in verbal discussions. Our consumption patterns may announce what we are worth, but specific discussions about money are still as off limits today as discussions about sex were in the 1950s. People seldom discuss their financial situation unless it is a matter of public record, and even then they tend to be closemouthed about what they do with their money. While we may have a general idea of an assistant professor's salary or the range within a salary grade, people seldom reveal specific figures. General discussions may take place among people who know they are in the same economic situation and share the same problems or circumstances, but quite often that depends on external information about one another's earnings.

Even husbands and wives, especially those who maintain separate finances, may not know their spouse's exact income. One man was startled when I asked him what he earned and said, "Gee, you know, I have never told anyone what I make, not even my wife." Other individuals revealed this information only after I reassured them of its confidentiality, and many wanted assurance that other respondents had been willing to divulge their incomes. Ironically, almost all these people were proud of what they earned and talked at length about the systems they had devised for sharing expenses, their lack of financial worries, and their attitudes toward money. Yet they did not know how others "did it," and they wanted me to tell them about other couples' financial arrangements. Many respondents began discussions about money by saying, "This may sound like a weird system . . ." or "Well, maybe we are a little different or strange, but . . ." This exchange of information sometimes became the basis on which people were willing to reveal financial matters.

Money remains a taboo issue for many couples because when people talk about money, they are simultaneously talking about authority relations. Authority relations reflect how much people earn, and the form of budgeting symbolizes how power is distributed in the family. If the questions of how money should be handled and, more important, why one person should make decisions about how it will be used are never confronted directly, authority relations can remain hidden or obscured. But when women earn as much as or more than their husbands, these questions are more difficult to avoid and can stimulate change in gender roles and authority relations between husbands and wives. When each partner has an income, they both are more likely to develop substantial autonomy. Husbands and wives with independent incomes may not necessarily create new methods for handling family financial affairs, but the possibility is available to them.

### *Accounting Systems*

The development of new familial accounting systems is an empirical indicator of a change in authority relations between husbands and wives. Lillian Rubin (1976) contrasts the importance of money and its management for working-class and professional middle-class families:

> Observers of American family life often point to the fact that so many women handle the family finances as evidence that they wield a great deal of power and influence in the family. A look *behind* that bare fact, however, suggests some other conclusions. Among the professional middle-class families, for example, where median income is $22,000—a level that allows for substantial discretionary spending—the figures flip over almost perfectly; the *men* manage the money in three-quarters of the families. Moreover, among those working-

> class families where some discretion in spending exists, almost always the husband handles the money, or the wife pays the bills while he makes the decisions. . . . Conversely, in the few professional families where the women manage the money, almost invariably they are families just beginning the climb upward—incomes are still quite low, and the choices around spending are very limited. . . . It seems reasonable to conclude, then, that men manage the money when there is enough of it so that the task involves some real decision-making (107–108).

For dual-career couples, however, the amount of discretionary income is no longer a simple determinant of which spouse makes decisions or which partner pays the bills. Instead, the restructuring of the accounting system—specifically, the autonomous use of discretionary money—may question men's traditional authority over familial decision making.

Accounting systems are a relevant measure of authority, because who is in charge of this system (or who handles the money) determines how money will be used and what investments will be made. Decisions about the use of money reflect relative authority in determining family lifestyle, comfort, and sense of worth—both with respect to maintenance of the family (how money is portioned out to pay for various things) and to individual self-worth. Further, resources and status acquired outside the family become the basis of authority to manage and distribute resources within the family.

Among the couples interviewed in this study, two basic accounting systems prevail: *separate* and *pooled.* Of twenty-one couples, eleven (or roughly 52 percent) maintain separate accounting systems. In households with such systems, the couple computes basic expenses, and each spouse contributes a set amount of money, either a share proportionate to income or an equal contribution despite income disparities, to a common "pot." In some cases, one spouse (regardless of gender) pays the bills; in others, the responsibility rotates. Some couples skip the step of placing money in a household account and instead divide up the actual amount needed to pay the bills, again doing so either proportionately or equally. (For example, one spouse may pay the mortgage and childcare expenses, which equal all other expenses.) Each partner keeps the remaining income in a separate account, to spend at his or her own discretion.

Ten of twenty-one couples (roughly 48 percent) maintain pooled accounting systems. In these cases, households put all income in joint accounts. Spouses may have separate business expense accounts or charge cards, and some have minimal "allowance" money. In this model, however, couples do not distinguish between collective and individual money. Instead, all income is collective regardless of who earns what proportion of it. Most commonly, the husband has primary responsibility for paying the bills; the major exception occurs when the wife's career involves financial expertise.[3]

The separate accounting system can be conceptualized as a model based on inflows of cash, where the partners divide between them the expenses of maintaining the household. If they decide to remodel or enlarge their home, for example, each spouse agrees to contribute additional money to the joint expense. First, however, each spouse must decide whether to contribute additional money to enhance some aspect of the collective lifestyle or to spend that money independently. The

3. Although I expected to find that couples with children would be more likely to have a communal or pooled accounting system, this was not the case. Of those couples who pooled their incomes, three had no children and eight had children. Of those couples who had a separate accounting system, four had no children and six had children.

TABLE 8. Type of Family Accounting System by Relative Income of Wife

| | *Pooled* | *Separate* | N |
|---|---|---|---|
| Wife higher | 33.3% | 66.7% | 6 |
| Wife equal[a] | 40.0% | 60.0% | 5 |
| Wife lower | 60.0% | 40.0% | 10 |
| Total | 47.6% | 52.4% | |
| N | 10 | 11 | 21 |

[a]Equal is defined as earning within $5,000 of one's spouse's income.

family, then, may be seen as a productive unit, and the individual spouses as distinctive consumers.

In the pooled accounting system, by contrast, the model is based on outflows of cash. External goods are transformed into familial rather than individual goods. (For example, items bought for the house are referred to as "our" possessions, not as "his" antique grandfather clock and "her" oriental rug.)

On the surface, these two models may appear to be simply two minor variations in approaches to household accounting. However, as Table 8 indicates, there appears to be a relationship between the relative earnings of spouses and the type of accounting system they devise. Although the size of the sample here is small, one finding is highly suggestive: families in which wives earn as much as or more than their husbands tend to employ separate accounting systems, whereas pooled accounting systems are more common when wives make less than their husbands.

The explanation for this apparent correlation, I believe, resides in the link between economic roles and the distribution of authority in the family. Men have traditionally derived their authority from status and resources acquired outside the family and have transformed that status and those resources into authority within the family. In the separate accounting model, wives act like their husbands, translating external status into familial authority. In this case, participation by both spouses in activities external to the family produces a more egalitarian family model. Put simply, the separate accounting system is an internal representation of extra-familial roles. In the pooled model, by contrast, female participation in the labor force may not alter the traditional familial authority structure. This model attempts to minimize the external inequality of the labor market (income disparities due either to industrial pay-scale differences or to level of career development) by pooling resources. More to the point, this collective familial model limits the autonomy of one or both spouses.[4]

Understanding the origin of these arrangements is the key to understanding money as an expression of the underlying authority relations between husbands and wives. In working-class families, arguments about money have to do with limited purchasing power or the lack of money—"coming up short" at the end of the month. Dual-career couples argue instead about the "rights" to that money. They ask who has the right to determine how the income will be spent, if both husband and wife are perceived as significant and central breadwinners. One woman, married four years, addressed this question:

> When we decided to get married, we had a very, very financial-type discussion. You know, where neither of us

4. Praeger (1982) discusses conflicts between individualistic and shared principles in marital property law, arguing that the individualistic model rewards self-interested choices that can be detrimental to marriage. Praeger argues for what I call the pooled system.

> wanted to give up the right to go out—like I'll go out and spend $400 on a suit and I don't want to hear about it; and Bill the same thing—he'll go to Florida and spend $1,000 on golf and he doesn't want to hear about it. So we both knew that we had to have enough money on our own, and this seemed like the fair way to do it.

The older notions of marriage—the merging of two individuals' resources based on unlimited trust—are now being questioned by couples who use separate accounting systems. It is not that they question who should have authority over money; rather, they feel that neither one should have authority over the other's money. When I asked how he and his wife came up with their present financial arrangement, the husband of the woman quoted above replied:

> Cindy and I tend to have the same view of money, which means that we both want all the money that we can lay our hands on for ourselves. I don't trust her enough with my money, and she certainly doesn't trust me enough with her money. So therefore the only possible workable scheme was to set up some sort of joint-versus-individual bills and accounts so that things could be allocated and we would both be able to retain our money—our *own* money.

### *Separate Accounts: What Is Ours?*

Partners developed their personal spending habits and eccentricities while single. Those who married in their mid- to late twenties had large incomes prior to marriage and were not willing to compromise their individual tastes or to be held accountable to anyone else for their spending patterns. This description of separate versus joint bills illustrates the point:

> We definitely divide up bills between those which are joint bills and those which are individual bills. If my wife buys clothes, that's her bill. If I buy wine, that's my bill. If it is an electric bill, that's a joint bill. [Why is wine bought by you?] My wife could care less about wine, and I like expensive wine. Even though she might drink some of it, there's no question that the only reason it is in the house is because I like it. That's something I enjoy, and I want it around.

Another respondent explained:

> If somebody wants to go out and buy something really stupid—and we all do that—why should the other partner be upset by it? And the only reason they are is when it's *their* money going into it and it's not the stupid thing *they* wanted to buy. So if you work it out this way [meaning separate accounting systems], he can do what he wants and he feels better about it, and I can buy what I want.

And still another remarked:

> I didn't want to have any arguments about finances. And I also knew that I was going to spend a lot of money as soon as I got my hands on it. I didn't want to be accountable to Jack for the money I spent on clothes, particularly.

Some couples who now have separate accounts did not begin with this system. Instead, money arguments led to a shift in financial arrangements. Although the arguments provoked financial change, in each case the wife's career and increasing income were the real catalysts behind the change. One man described the outcome of money arguments this way:

> We got tired of arguing about money, and we decided we would try having a third account that would just be fair game for all those things that were joint household accounts. For example, I don't pay for any of the clothing she gets, and the joint account doesn't pay for any either. . . .

> [What were you arguing about in terms of money?] Well, she would go out and buy herself a new blouse or something like that, and I'd say, "You've already got a thousand blouses. What did you need a new blouse for?" and I would go on harping. She'd say, "Oh, I need a new blouse," or something like that.

One woman suggested that prior to creating a separate accounting system, she had felt doubly penalized: her discretionary income subsidized her husband's desires, while his spending habits impeded decisions about collective expenditures.

> We decided jointly to remodel the house. . . . I don't care what he does with his account. I don't care about what he buys. If he wants to go out and buy $150 worth of shirts, and that's what he wants to do with his money, that's fine. But before, *I* was subsidizing that. And it was very distressing when I was trying to get money together to pay off a tradesman and he would go out and buy these sorts of things for himself. . . . His priorities are not my priorities. And there is nothing wrong with his having his priorities as long as it's not penalizing someone else or things we've decided to do jointly. But the way it was going [when we pooled our money], I felt I was being penalized. Now, if it's a fixed expenditure that we both agree upon, it will either come out of that account or we will both chip in additional money to that account. The rest of the remodeling has gone smoother, and what he buys with his own money no longer bothers me.

Another woman, who felt that her husband was spending most of the discretionary income on himself and leaving little for her, finally spoke to female friends at work about their financial arrangements with their spouses and discovered that she was "getting screwed." After ten years of pooling all their income, she and her husband decided on a separate accounting system.

> [The money] was all in one joint account, and I found that I was always coming up short. And I figured that I was busting my tail at work and at home and that I should have money left for me. I didn't at all. . . . Over the years my discretionary income was subsidizing his expense account at his office, and I finally decided, "Nope, you can sink on your own." Now it is wonderful I have *that* income. And now he says, "How am I going to pay my half of the Marshall Field's bill?" and I say, "It's your problem. Here's a check for my half of the bill."

With less money held collectively, the amount controlled by each individual wage earner increases. Pooling all income may mean in theory that both partners have discretionary authority over money; but, as the comments quoted above imply, one partner may feel that money not needed for household essentials is being spent at his or her expense or at the expense of the family. Pooling only fixed expenses—the money necessary for running the household—thus curtails individual discretion about the spending of pooled income. For example, instead of one spouse making decisions about $5,000 of discretionary income, each partner has decision power about $2,500. In separate accounting systems, women are asserting the same authority over discretionary income that men have traditionally had. In essence, these couples are reducing the conflict over who has legitimate claims to discretionary income.

Unlike couples who use pooled accounting systems, the couples with separate accounting systems confront money matters head-on; they have chosen to settle the issue of differential claims to money based on differential incomes through their separate financial accounting system. In the majority of cases, they base equity between husbands and wives on a proportionate contribution to the collective account. When I asked why they decided on a proportionate rather than an equal contribution to the collective account, couples said it was "fair" or "more equitable to give each of us financial freedom." This system also means that couples are reducing the effects of inequities in pay between different types of industries as well as between different career stages in the same industry. When one spouse had more savings at the beginning of the marriage, these couples even attempted to equalize savings. The following example illustrates one of the more complicated calculations:

> What we do is take our gross salaries. Then we basically say, "Okay, I have a life insurance payment. That's to her benefit." So I subtract that out before we come down to the amount agreed to go into the joint account. She has a life insurance payment, which she subtracts out. She has a disability insurance payment, which she subtracts because I'm covered. We agree that she can have x amount per month for lunch, because I get a free lunch, so that sort of equalizes the salaries in terms of contributions. We agreed upfront that her student loans ought to be paid off, so this comes from up-front money before we do the division. We agreed that she should be saving money up to a certain amount to bring her up to a comfortable level of compensation cash in case she wants to quit—so she doesn't have to fall back on me to do so. I already have a certain amount of savings from an earlier period. All those things come out of her and my gross salaries.

Another respondent, who makes less than her husband, keeps records of what she owes him for his contributing more money to the household than she can afford to do on her present income. Further, she kept financial records during the time he supported her through school, a practice that was important for her own self-esteem. She hopes to pay off the debt in the future.

I like to keep things tidy. So I've kept records of how much I might owe him for certain periods of time. Now that I'm working, although we're not making the same income, I feel we should split our obligations. So if we spend more than I could afford, and hence he's contributing more to make it work, then I just tally it up and keep a running ledger of this sort of thing.

Andy was very generous in terms of giving me a lot of time to think out what I wanted to do—what job I wanted to take and all of that—and he supported me. But in terms of my own feelings of self-esteem and being a contributor, I would keep records of anything he gave me for support so that at some point in my life, we'd be able to even it out.

What couples do with discretionary income affects their collective lifestyle. One partner may be a spendthrift and the other a miser. What happens, for example, when a couple decides to make a substantial investment, such as buying a larger condominium or purchasing a new car? Or what happens when the value of one partner's investments increases faster? The following quote best captures the way in which most couples view separate investments. This couple places their first-of-the-month paychecks in the joint account and their mid-month paychecks in their individual accounts:

When my husband or I invest in something, he thinks of it and I think of it as being mutually owned. But the fact is, we try to keep a certain amount of control through separate accounts. I guess it probably alleviates a lot of the questions about making decisions on how much money to save and what we're going to do with it. The results are going to affect us both. I mean, if we need to have another apartment and he has all the savings, he's the one who's going to be putting down the down payment because he makes more money. So we view investments as mutual.

The "playing" may be individual but the net result is joint. With few exceptions, people placed investments in both their names or willed the partner all such holdings. In addition, they put some investments in their children's names.

A separate accounting system accommodates different attitudes about money, so that couples do not have to agree about either the value of money or how to spend it. However, partners do not necessarily approve of or ignore different values.

> Burt is much more compulsive in terms of money management than I am. He balances his checkbook and I never do. When my bills come in the mail, he gets terribly annoyed if I don't pay them on time. It's just not part of me to pay bills on time. . . . He likes things orderly, and I like to do things my way.

In this case the conflict of different styles of bill paying was resolved by the wife writing her own checks on time and the husband mailing the bills and handling the paperwork.

Partners' different attitudes toward money, as described in the following story, illustrate how the miser-spendthrift dichotomy can be one source of conflict:

> I'm the much greater believer in leverage, particularly during inflationary periods, and my husband is much more conservative. He saves everything and sees that it all builds up nicely so he'll have something to take care of him. That money will go "zippo" if inflation continues. The purchasing power is going to be next to nothing. I have a much different attitude toward money—what I do with my money and how I live my life—than my husband does. He's more of a saver, and I tend to lever myself more. He doesn't like it, and I tell him, "Tough. I'm not asking you to support me."

Her husband's story is slightly different. He invests his discretionary money, and she spends hers. Although the investments are labeled his, they are held in joint tenancy. As he said, "It's a bone of contention. She won't save. But I save, and I invest it. But it is all in her name, as it turns out."

These contrasting attitudes toward money are not necessarily gender-related. A wife who believes in saving money for long-term investments, and whose husband believes in buying on credit, feels that the difference stems from different family backgrounds:

> My husband was raised in a credit-card atmosphere, with his father owning a portion of a large company at the time when tax laws were really pretty loose. So, they were just able to take advantage of a lot of things that I think led to easier money styles than we had in my house. In my family's home, everything was saved, and then you had the money to buy what you wanted.

## MONEY AND INDEPENDENCE

Being able to support oneself is a crucial element of independence. A woman's choice to remain in an existing marriage or to be married at all no longer needs to be based on the financial considerations that a nonexistent or low-paying job might have imposed. Money, as this woman testified, makes a difference for dual-career wives in that it places women on an equal footing with men:

> I'm in the relationship because I want to be, not because somebody's taking care of me. If I want to take a walk, I can take a walk and not worry about being able to take care of myself. From my viewpoint it certainly does give me some independence. I feel like I don't have to say, "Well, you're bringing in the money that's putting food on the table, that's keeping me alive." I'm putting in money, too.

Money—specifically, two substantial incomes—also allows for career change, and it liberates individuals from being the sole financial provider for the family. In the following example, one woman described the conditions under which she would (hypothetically) be willing to sacrifice their present level of income and lifestyle:

> If he were to say to me, "It is really very important to me to go back to school to get an M.B.A. or a Ph.D. in whatever; can we make it?" I would probably say yes. Not probably, I would most definitely say yes. That to me is a goal-oriented activity. You know, if I have to live on a budget, sell the house, and really bust my ass for two years because it is really important to him and he's going someplace, then everybody will sort of pull together because we have to do that. But for him to come to me and say, "You know, we could probably live on *only* your salary. I don't want to work"—no way.

This sentiment is shared by husbands about their wives. In these marriages, no one gets a free financial ride. Yet both husbands and wives are willing to invest in the other partner as long as the investment is goal-oriented (getting more education, starting an independent business). Another wife, who made more than her husband, kept pushing him to take a career risk, not only because he wanted to make more money but also because they could live on her salary:

> I keep encouraging him to go out and do something on his own: "It may be risky, but we can pay our bills with my salary. You should go do something risky. Let me hold down the fort, and if you lose money, who cares? We won't starve."

Other spouses had supported their partners for several years while one spouse returned to school, changed his or her occupation, or established a business. As one husband explained:

> I think Lisa probably feels she made a significant investment in terms of my building this business. If it weren't for her income, which we lived on, and her encouragement, this couldn't have happened. That is a direct example of the freedom I have had because of my wife's income. Because of the investment on her part, she likes to know what is going on with this business.

One woman, who initially worked only for financial reasons, explained how her present earnings were important not only for freeing her husband from sole financial responsibility for the family but also for the lifestyle they have become accustomed to:

> My income is not a supplement anymore. It's a big chunk of money. It's what a guy with two kids has to support his whole family on. It's a lot of money to just remove from your way of life. As my income gets larger, it makes it more difficult to get rid of it; and therefore it's not a supplement. It makes a big difference in our lives. . . . But it has been one-sided in that my working has always given my husband freedom from financial worries, which allowed him freedom to come and go in terms of job mobility.

Couples who have chosen separate accounting systems have made a distinction between collective money and individual money. Their "money consciousness" is very different from that of couples who have pooled accounting systems.

### *Pooled Money: His, Hers, or Theirs?*

Why have some couples chosen to pool their incomes and others chosen to distinguish "my money" from "your money"? Do they have different attitudes toward their marital relationships, and do they have different attitudes toward money? My findings indicate that husbands and wives who have pooled accounting systems view their financial arrangements as an outgrowth of a more traditional orientation toward marriage. In addition, the wives of these couples lack a "money fluency" in discretionary expenditures. In the majority of cases, the husbands take care of finances. Their wives tend to be squeamish about money—not wanting to understand financial matters even when husbands want them to be active participants. By choosing to remain ignorant, these women absolve themselves of financial responsibilities, and they forsake the authority vested in the person who exercises control over finances. A few husbands have kept their wives in the dark about finances, refusing to reveal or discuss money issues with them. Their wives were frustrated, angry, and bitter, claiming that their husbands were "undercutting their financial earnings." In both cases, because the issue of money is not confronted, the wife's paycheck has only a limited effect on altering traditional authority relations and the division of labor within the household.

### *Traditional Views of Marriage*

Compared to couples who use separate accounting systems, couples who pool their money have a more traditional orientation toward marriage, conceptualizing it as a merger of two individuals, based on "mutual dependence" and "unlimited trust." As one wife explained, "We have a sharing of everything that goes on. Our relationship is built on mutual dependence. There has never been a situation where Sam said he wouldn't let me do something or buy something." The pooled accounting system is an extension of this idea of a merger. According to the woman quoted above, "There is no identification of my money versus his money." Another woman stated, "We have a joint account. It's our money." An independent income alone does not give these respondents a sense of independence, freedom, or great influence over decision making in the home. A larger combined income has led to less concern about individual spending but has not eliminated the need to justify making purchases for individual use. This situation is reflected in the comments of a female respondent:

> The freedom comes from having so much more money put together now. Before, I never went to him when I wanted to buy something. But I didn't buy it because I didn't think we could afford it. For example, I like to buy clothes every once in a while, and I used to feel uncomfortable about it because I would stretch our budget, or so Jim thought. And I think I agreed with him about clothes periodically. Now, two incomes combined allow me to go out and buy something that I just wouldn't have bought before.

Couples who pool their money have a propensity for a traditional gender-based division of labor, characterized by traditional separate "spheres of influence" in the home. One husband's comments illustrate this traditional model:

> We have got our own little spheres of influence—like I do the bookkeeping that we have, handling the finances. Ann will help out in terms of keeping track of the finances, although I take principal responsibility there. And she takes principal responsibility in the kitchen. She also supervises the administration of running the household, you know, managing the housekeeper.

Pooling incomes implies an attempt to avoid highlighting or distinguishing between the incomes of husbands and wives. It is one way to avoid the conversations and confrontations about discrepancies in income faced by couples who choose separate accounting systems. This respondent avoids confronting her husband with the fact that she earns and contributes more to their pooled income:

> A couple of times I've said, when he's not been excited that I have to work on a Saturday, "I have to work late. I'm earning my bonus." I don't say, "I'm earning that extra." I don't even know how much—well, it could be $35,000. I could be making almost double his salary this year. I don't say, "I have to work harder because I get paid more," either.

Although she does not confront him directly, she does acknowledge to herself that she makes more money. And because she makes more, even though the money is pooled she lays claim to that money in ways that women who earn less are not about to do; that is, she plans to spend some of it the way she wants, despite her husband's disapproval. In this case, she wants to help a sibling financially. She explained her dilemma:

> I don't even know if I have said it to him, but I feel like I make a lot more, and so if I want to do that with some extra money and it's not hurting him and it's helping my sister out, I ought to do it. I haven't gotten to the bottom of why that bothers him, but I feel it's my right to do. I work hard and I'll do whatever I want to. . . . So I've got to decide whether to tell John that I'm sending her more money, when I just sent her $300 last month. He'd never have to know, but I'll probably tell him. He'll get mad. But still, I don't make a big thing about making more, and I'll do what I want. I just say that I feel I should send her the money.

She remains very conscious of the fact that she earns more; her husband explained the gap as a "discrepancy because of the type of industry," not because of career status.

Even though she once handled her own money, another woman writes off her husband's handling of the finances as a "tradition" within their marriage:

> I really don't know how it got started, because I had a brief period in college when I had some money and I handled it myself. But when we got married, we were both working. I really wasn't working any more overtime than he was, but he just started handling the finances and he continued to. When I wasn't working for a while, I'd help him pay bills, but even then I didn't do much. "Help" meant that he was still the main person. I think it's tradition within our marriage.

Many of these women have opted to limit their involvement with financial matters. Husbands balance their checkbooks, decide whether there is money for a particular purchase, and make the investment decisions. It is important to understand the attitudes of these women toward money, as it may offer a key to understanding why authority relations for these couples remain unaltered. Women give a variety of reasons and rationalizations for either not wanting to know about money or their unwillingness to discuss it. One woman, disinterested in their finances, trusted her husband with her money:

> As a matter of fact, I'm not 100 percent sure how much money my husband makes. I'm sure he would tell me; it's just that I never asked. You know, I trust him completely when he makes up this budget. He makes up this little chart, and he always wants to tell me exactly what's going on. But all I really want to know is the bottom line, and it always seems like a reasonable amount, so I don't worry about it. I think he gets paid every other week like I do. So if I wanted to look at it, I could.

This woman, who did not know what her husband made, admitted, "I'm not exactly sure how much he makes—about $55,000, I think. He can tell you. I don't know exactly what he makes. I always forget, and right now it's embarrassing me." Another woman explained the sense of awe surrounding money by describing what she does when she receives her paycheck:

> When I get my paycheck, I touch it. We've got a system whereby it can automatically be put in the bank, and I refuse to do it. It makes my husband mad, because we lose interest on it. And I say to him that I like to look at it. . . . He handles the finances, so I just give it to him, to be honest. It sounds like I'm being a baby. He puts it either in checking or savings, because he follows that much more closely than I do.

She is fascinated with the fact that she earns this check. Yet beyond that, her husband not only balances her checkbook but also manages the finances.

Another woman, who until age twenty-nine was single and earning a healthy income, attributed her lack of money management to a strong aversion to money. Again, she trusts her husband to take care of it.

> I am very, very bad with money. I owe everybody in the world. I mean, I charge, charge, charge, and I never record my checks. I was miserable and I hated [managing money] and I still hate it. So he handles all the money. I have an idea what kind of money we have, but I know he is not going to screw me. I know that I am a strong enough person that, God forbid something happens, I could get it together like that [snaps her fingers]. I know our lawyers. I know the key things. I don't care about the rest. I could give a damn. So he handles all the money—total and complete.

Yet ironically, although this woman has a distaste for the details of money management at home, later on in the interview she revealed a different attitude toward entertaining business clients in the presence of her husband: "The business involves so much night entertaining—all of which he comes to if he can. He loves it. And he is my husband there. I sign the checks."

Having a distaste for money is analogous to women having mental blocks against math. It is striking that almost all these women have managerial or higher positions in the business world. With few exceptions, they all hold advanced degrees, mostly M.B.A.s. Yet, they are not interested in the gamesmanship of money, nor do they understand money management. Instead of confronting financial issues, they have retreated behind their husbands' cloaks. By convincing themselves that they are not interested in money, these women continue to mystify finances and deny that money is important.

This woman explained her discomfort with bill paying as a "psychological problem"—an aversion to risk taking:

> So we've gotten into a system, at this point, where every month I figure out how much money I need to live on, and then I just write him a check for the rest. And then he pays whatever bills and puts the rest aside. I've always had a psychological problem with bills. I don't pay bills, either. I don't open my checking account statements except like once every three months. I'll balance my checkbook every quarter.
>
> He doesn't go off and invest money without telling me or asking me what I think we ought to do. It is just now that I'm starting to be able to take an active role in that, and that's because of my risk profile. You know, I worry a lot about risk. Years ago, for a long time, I couldn't even write the rent checks. Back in 1972 we were paying $285 for rent, which seems low now, but then it was a lot. God, every time I had to write the rent check I'd nearly faint. But now I am able to take a more active role.

She believes she will be able to participate more fully in financial affairs in the future. She talked about her change in attitude:

> It's just a level of affluence and a level of comfort. You reach a certain level, where you know you're not going to starve to death and that you're going to be able to pay the dentist and stuff like that. Also, you begin to become more comfortable with your earning power. Just in terms of my own self-confidence, it's only been in the last two-and-a-half years that I've really been able to feel good about myself.

Her husband would like her input:

> I don't think Ellen would mind if I went ahead and did all this stuff without consulting her, really. But I do consult her. She has never initiated an investment idea. I'd like her to have some good investment ideas—better than the ones I've had. . . . We decide how to carve up our money—buy stocks or tax shelters, and so on. We discuss all that together, and we have done some things that were initiated by me and acquiesced to by her.

Another woman described her own feelings about money in a disinterested tone:

> I really don't have any knowledge about what's a good investment—this kind of tax shelter, this kind of bond. I'm not sure I have the interest to learn. I mean, I would like to be more familiar with it, and yet I have not gotten off my ass to go and really take a course and become a bit more intelligent. Don, on the other hand, because of where he works and because he took some courses in real estate and finance—he's just more knowledgeable. We talk about things. But basically, to put it in this tax shelter or, I don't know, this bond or that—it's basically his decision. And I'm not sure how I feel about it. I guess I'm not uncomfortable, because I would have done something about it.

Her husband was not pleased with her attitude. He wished the financial burdens were shared, and commented,

> We don't have many investments, and we don't talk about them as much as I would like. I went to a weekend seminar on real estate investment a year ago. I wanted Lee to come, and she didn't want to go. So she didn't. With two of us working, both of us are short on time. It makes it harder for one person to have to be responsible for all the reading or whatever you have to do when it comes to investing. This is part of why we haven't done as much investing as I think we should.

Quite commonly, these women did spend money without their husbands' consent. Yet, at least one respondent wanted validation from her husband when she spent a lot of money on herself:

> I have to be honest with you. I bought a Nipon dress. And it was about $250. I didn't buy it until I discussed it with my husband, because the price shocked me. But it was the one thing I liked, and you know what he said?—"Why did you ask me?" But I didn't stop there. Then I said, "Well, you come down and see it." What finally dawned on me was that in my mind it was such an incredible purchase that I wanted a validation from him. I dragged him to Handmoor's, and he was so bored. . . . He didn't even look at the dress. He just said, "Goddamn it, buy it."

Another respondent is one of the two wives who earn more than their husbands and also pool incomes. Her reasons for pooling resources are interesting, especially as the tendency is not to pool when wives earn more. Although she acknowledges that other people might know that she makes more than her husband, she prefers to keep it a "family secret." Perhaps she fears emasculating her husband publicly, and she does not need or want to emasculate him privately, either; by pooling her larger income, she is able to think of it as *their* money, not her money.

> It's not really that bad an issue for us that I make more. I mean, we don't go around telling people about it. I've had friends who, not from their salaries but from their families' money, had a lot more from the wife's side; and the wife will say, "That's my car and my house." I don't ever say that to anybody—that I make more than my husband. Some people, I'm sure—because they know general salaries at the company I work for and at the company my husband works for—must figure I do make more. But we don't mention it. I just don't make it an issue, and it doesn't bother him.

## CONCLUSION

The mere fact of women earning independent incomes has not necessarily led to a revolutionary change in authority relations between husbands and wives. What happens to that income and how respondents view it become equally important. A correlation seems to exist between the type of accounting system used by dual-career couples and the authority relations within their marriages. In general, those couples who have chosen separate accounting systems have made a step toward altering the traditional balance of marital authority. Having money has allowed the development of substantial autonomy for each spouse: the individual is no longer subject to collective discretion, nor must he or she seek the approval of the other, dominant, spouse; autonomy is gained by the expenditure of individual income. The structure of the accounting system questions the traditional authority of men to make familial decisions and allows women to assert the same authority over discretionary income that men have had in the past. In contrast, when pooled accounting systems have been selected, authority relations between husbands and wives seem to have undergone only limited change. Wives in these relationships absolved themselves of financial responsibilities. Thus, the existence of two incomes itself does not make the crucial difference; rather, the mechanisms devised to deal with this money should provide the focal point for studying husband-wife relations in dual-career couples.

Nevertheless, one of the balancing factors in marriage is having money. An independent income also represents a certain stage in one's career, so that career and money together are significant influences on major family decisions. One of the most crucial decisions related to the "third career"—marriage—and its viability involves having children. And yet a significant aspect of having a career is its continuity—the lack of major lapses of time spent within an organization or in the continuous process of acquiring more skill or experience. For dual-career couples, as we shall see in the next chapter, the question of whether or not to have children directly challenges the concept of conjoining two careers and, necessarily, the independence associated with separate and equal sources of income.

# 4

# HAVING CHILDREN: Decisions, Strategies, and Constraints

As ARGUED earlier, corporate organizations have a tremendous influence on the personal lives of their employees. How and where employees live, whether they extend their education, how much free (nonwork) time they have, and how they socialize are all structured by the employing organization. Few corporations would deny that they have such pervasive effects, but even fewer would accept total responsibility for them. Most organizations are seen as a hierarchy of positions: a structure of demands and opportunities that define a ladder of career development and promotion. Access to and movement up that ladder require that individual employees make choices about investments in education and training and about the rewards for commitment and stability. Although organizations and their leaders may arbitrarily set or change the rules for access and mobility, the choice to invest or to stay is made by the individual and is presumably in keeping with his or her own preferences.

One intensely personal area of employees' lives has become increasingly affected by organizational demands, however: the decision to have or not to have children. The relationship between organizational and career-based demands, on the one hand, and decisions about having children, on the other, was traditionally muted by the dominance of men in corporate and professional jobs and by the preponderance of one-career households. Although some employers may have considered married men with children to be a guarantee of employee stability and may have encouraged children by providing medical benefits for dependents, the question of whether a couple would have children was much less affected by the organization and by careers than by other facets of personal life. The traditional division of labor in the family allowed husbands to work outside the home continuously, while wives bore and cared for children. Dual-career couples, however, cannot make decisions about children as easily. Two sets of organizational and career demands are brought into conflict by the prospect of even temporary withdrawal of one partner from a career and by the subsequent problem of managing childcare. Career aspirations must be reconciled with both personal and social expectations about what constitutes a proper family.

This chapter examines how dual-career couples deal with the question of having children and specifically how organizations and career demands influence such decision making. The influence of a less obvious set of factors stemming from their views of the woman's role in the family—namely, the importance of children and the relative importance of each spouse's career—is also assessed. While it is difficult to disentangle preexisting views of gender roles and family from those created by organizational demands, a close examination of the circumstances faced by couples in this sample shows the relationship between attitudes and behaviors. To gain an understanding of the process of making decisions about children, the following questions are explored: (1) How do organizations and careers influence decisions about the feasibility or the timing of children? (2) Is there a contradiction between career success and the social expectations about women's role as mothers? (3) Do efforts by dual-career couples to strike a balance between family and career result in any significant changes in gender roles?

## WORK DEMANDS

Couples both with and without children were interviewed for this study. As can be seen in Table 9, one difference between those couples with children and

TABLE 9. Men's and Women's Ages and Desire to Have Children

| | *With Children* | *Without Children* |
|---|---|---|
| Percentage of sample (N = 20)[a] | 65% | 35% |
| Average age (men/women) | 36.2/34.9 | 34.1/31.6 |
| Average age at birth of first child (men/women)[b] | 31.4/30.2 | — |
| Desire to have children | — | 85% |

[a]One couple has been omitted from these figures; in their case, the husband's children from a previous marriage reside with the couple. Although this couple has had no children together and are not likely to have any in the future, in all other chapters they are included in the category of those with children because their lifestyle is affected by the children's presence.

[b]Another man in this sample had children by a former marriage, but the children do not reside with this couple. Age at the birth of the first child in his current marriage is indicated here. No women in this study had children with former spouses.

those without is age: couples with children were slightly older than those without. However, the average age of women at the birth of their first child was slightly lower than the average age at the time of the interview of women without children. The majority of women with children had had them in their late twenties or early thirties; two women had children in their early twenties, prior to shifting their careers from other fields to business.[1] Like all the other women with children in this study, these women continued to work while their children were young. Women without children were interviewed at the time when they were confronting the difficult decisions about having children. Only one couple had already decided not to have children; they were the oldest in the group. The remainder hoped to have children soon. For some this meant within the year; others intended to wait until the wife's thirty-fifth birthday.

Husbands and wives' decisions about when to have children and how to rear them involve complex calculations concerning career goals and the couple's projected future lifestyle. On an individual level, the type of job and its demands, the stage of one's career, its potential for mobility, and one's career goals all impinge on the decision to have children. (For the couple, projected lifestyle would include income, quality of life, and so on.)

The couples I interviewed invested heavily in careers following graduate school and established lifestyles in which work was the central activity. Prior to having children, both husband and wife were equally active in pur-

1. According to the U.S. Bureau of the Census (1983, 1–2), the fertility rate among women thirty to thirty-four years old rose 22.5 percent, from 60 births per 1,000 in 1980 to 73.5 births per 1,000 in 1982. The increase in the fertility rate of women in their early thirties that began in the mid-1970s has apparently continued into the 1980s and reflects a change toward having children later in life.

suing their individual careers and establishing themselves in their respective fields. Although focusing on academia, Hochschild (1971, 1975) argues that the normative view of professional careers is based on a masculine prototype for both professional and family life; the couples in this sample followed a similar pattern. Family obligations are minimized and scarce time is hoarded; for instance, couples often work late in their respective offices, leaving a home routine and schedule subject to last-minute alterations. One respondent outlined the arrangements he and his wife made to ensure separate career investments:

> Generally, one of us or both of us are working late. So it's totally unpredictable who's going to be home when. We're both home by eight o'clock 90 percent of the time. However, I think we both work until we best get a hand on whatever we're doing at the time; and if that means working until seven o'clock, eight o'clock, or nine o'clock on a particular day, we don't hesitate to do it. In this sense there isn't any pressure to be home at a particular time. . . . I don't think either of us expects the other to be home much before seven o'clock or so as a routine, and there are always going to be regular exceptions—that is, nine or ten o'clock. You don't know what they are or when they are, but you just realize that in any five days, you're going to work until ten o'clock one of those days.

Unfortunately, as Hochschild points out, the time of intensive career building coincides with the traditional time for building a family. Therefore, having children is commonly postponed during this time of joint career investment. In contrast, for couples where only the husband has a career, the classic pattern is the simultaneous timing of two events: his first job and her first pregnancy.

For dual-career couples, long hours at the office and business-related traveling reduce the amount of time the partners have to spend together and act as a further impetus to postponing children. At some point in their careers, the majority of husbands and wives in the sample worked in jobs that entailed heavy national or international travel. Client-oriented jobs that involve working on accounts, projects, and other detailed transactions require a great deal of time away from home, especially if the client is located out of town. Consulting firms are the most visible examples of corporate work that requires trips, but other jobs in a variety of fields, such as advertising and marketing, also involve extensive travel. Travel time and the unpredictability of assignments make it difficult to establish a lifestyle that can accommodate the demands of young children. A woman who does not have children described her schedule:

> I figured out how much travel I did for the first three years with this corporation, and I haven't figured it out since. I travel about a third of the time, but that varies a lot. The first year I traveled 12 percent, the second year I traveled about 55 or 59 percent, and the third year about 29 percent. It averaged out to be about a third. . . . My husband travels as much as I do.

To explain the variability in his travel, one man without children detailed the schedule of the past two summers:

> Last summer I was commuting to London. So I'd be in London a week and come home a week, and then go to London for a week and come home for a week. This summer I haven't been gone that much. I went to Australia for a week, and I'll probably be going back again in August. There are also always one or two overnights here and there.

His wife, whose trips were minimal at the time, expected her next project assignment to involve extensive travel. In explaining travel schedules and work demands in general, she concluded, "We've been very lucky, because for one thing we don't have children to worry about."

For most jobs, travel requirements are not negotiable with the employer, and individuals have limited control over when they travel and where. As one husband explained:

> I can't schedule my travel so that I'll be gone at the same time my wife is gone. I handle a lot of financial transactions, and I have to go when the financers tell me to go. I don't have a choice, and it's the same when my wife is assigned a project.

To compound the problem, individuals are not in a position to select their clients or their projects until they accrue seniority within the organization. Turning down an assignment because it requires travel is perceived as dangerous to a career, as one woman noted about her consulting work:

> If I'm coming off one study and another one is starting up that's away from here, I don't have any choice but to accept it. [To turn it down is] pretty much unacceptable behavior. . . . Now, internationally there's always a choice. No one is asked to go abroad if he doesn't want to go, although some people perceive pressure to do that regardless, because our office manager here is very supportive of the international work as a broadening experience both professionally and personally. Everyone realizes that he thinks that, and to say no would put you in a somewhat unfavorable light.

Thus, work demands, whether self-imposed or structurally imposed, contribute to postponing children.

Although couples acknowledge the importance of disrupted household routines, demanding work schedules, and travel requirements for career building, the incompatibility of careers and children nonetheless generates a quiet resentment among some. Instead of collectively voicing these complaints and looking for solutions, however, they hope to solve this problem individually. One woman described her resentment:

> I want my work to be only a part of my life. One of the frustrations I have with this job is that it consumes so much of you, because of the long hours that we work and the travel. That's a resentment that I have against this kind of work. My other life has been consumed by it, and I don't want to be deprived entirely by my job.
>
> You know, the life I have just described to you—where do you put a child in there? There are some people who do try to do that, and I know some women that do have children, but they are very few and far between. Mostly, they don't stop and have children when they're in this business. There are people who got their graduate degrees at a later date. They had their children earlier; it's easier to figure out what to do with an eight-year-old than with a six-month-old.

A man summed up the problem this way:

> I see some couples that are going to have a lot of trouble. They don't have any children, and they are both in very demanding careers. See, I don't think you can have a family and have two demanding careers. I think someone has to give; otherwise there is no way it's going to work. I imagine it could work, but then I don't think you have any business having a kid. Most of the people I know—in several cases, both [spouses] are professionals, and it's the woman who has given it up.

## CAREER SUCCESS AND WOMEN AS MOTHERS

Most corporate careers are constructed around male social roles and experiences. Employers expect employees to invest themselves in their jobs, and they invest, in turn, in those who do. Yet, when career-oriented women decide to bear and care for children in a traditional fashion (such as taking time off from employment while the children are young) rather than following the stereotyped male career pattern, it is interpreted as a decision to *disinvest* in the organization. This interpretation is reflected in the minimal leaves allowed pregnant women and the costs in money and status they bear when they attempt to return after a prolonged absence. Women are told, in effect, that the path of least resistance is one charted according to a male model rather than a female model. Women come to recognize the cruel irony that the opportunity to have a career does "liberate" them from traditional roles and expected behavior, but at the same time the only real opportunity this freedom allows is for women to adopt a male career model.

Parents, older relatives, and influential traditionalists hold expectations about women's behavior toward children and childrearing that tend to push women in the opposite direction. The traditional attitude that investments in family and children should predominate over career investments and the general cultural milieu in which many couples were raised weigh heavily on women as they ponder their decisions about children. In addition, over the last twenty to thirty years a substantial portion of the research on women and labor force participation has focused on the impact of the mother's working on the child's development. Rarely has research investigated the impact of the father's working, with the notable exception of absentee fathers, who are generally considered deviant. The cumulative impact of family expectations, cultural milieu, and social science research has put continued pressure on women to be mothers and to perform in accepted social and familial roles. For some women the pressure is perceived as immutable; for most it is a force as significant in shaping their lives as the expectations of their employers.

Corporate accommodation to pregnancy did not exist in most firms fifteen or even ten years ago. One of the only women in this study to have had a child in her early twenties described the company attitude toward pregnant women ten years ago: "I don't even know if there were such things as leaves of absence for pregnant ladies back then. You just went away when you got pregnant, and they hoped you would never come back." The organizations in which these women worked had established few if any precedents for pregnancy among female managers. There were not many women role models in any of these corporations who had tested what would happen if they decided to have children; some women in this study were, in fact, among the highest ranking women in their respective corporations, and some had actually set the maternity policy in their company. For the most part the attitude among women without children was to wait and see what happened when women above them or in other parts of the same corporation had children. One summer intern did raise the question of children with her male boss. His response is typical of the male attitude of co-workers and superiors, as females perceive it. Another woman in the firm recounted the story:

> She got into a discussion with at least one man here, and his attitude was that it is totally impossible to have children and work here. . . . I think it is the work demand this company puts on your life in terms of hours and travel and this guy's perception. He has two children, and his wife dedicated her life to the children. So, it's his perception of what it takes for his wife and the way they set up their household—he puts two and two together, and he says it's impossible.

It is indicative of the sensitivity of this matter that an outsider, not a regular female employee, raised the question about pregnancy. Most of the women in this study viewed the issue as their own individual problem. No one spoke of a collective effort to solve the problem of integrating family and work. One woman said, "I have been afraid to ask. I don't want to raise it until it's *my* issue, instead of a general issue" [emphasis added].

The lack of collective effort or even of open discussion of pregnancy and childrearing as a women's issue may result from most of these women being among the "second stage" (Friedan, 1981) in the corporate world—the first wave having secured jobs at the expense of bearing children or having sacrificed careers for traditional mothering roles. Now, the major problem this current generation of women faces is wanting *both* careers and children. As long as these women remain childless, they feel that their male colleagues accept them as equals or "semimen." But traditional attitudes of male co-workers about the proper place of women with young children further confound the personal dilemma of how to simultaneously have a career and family, as this woman revealed:

> When I left, I was the second highest woman in the company. There were a lot of women by that time, and I've never felt that working with men is a big issue. I think the issue of me as a woman comes around having children rather than around working with men. The child thing is more of a problem because they have their attitude about how children should be raised—like they're doing it with their wives at home.

The career consequences of biological differences, even when maternity leaves are provided, are undeniable. Female respondents expressed concern that bearing children could jeopardize their careers even if they planned an immediate return following a maternity leave. One woman contended that women pay a long-term price for having children:

> If you're very concerned about your career, if you're into your own future potential, both in terms of where you're going and how much you're going to make and everything else, having a child is a tremendous career interruption. Children are still something which can never have a good impact on your career. It's just something you feel you have to apologize for. You know, if I were a man it wouldn't be a problem; but I'm a woman, so we do bear children . . . and it can take years to make up for the fact that you've had a child. It's like something that you've done to the corporation. You don't get rewards for doing things like this to the corporation; someone has to fill in for you when you're gone.

One woman, who railed against the separate and unequal treatment accorded men and women, described the impact maternity leaves can have on career progression:

> All of us know that having a child could mean the difference between getting a promotion and not getting a promotion. [How so?] You have to take a leave of absence. If you're not there, that's time somebody else has gained on you. You are functionally not part of the corporation when you're on leave, even if they are paying you. You can't gain time getting something in the year in which you have a child. I mean, that may be the only year for three years that something might come up that would mean you could get a promotion.

Ironically, work for some of these women did not abate entirely during maternity leaves. They reported continuing work, such as writing reports or making hiring decisions, in the hospital or at home. One woman admitted:

> I did my budget at home because it was due. What was I going to say—"Sorry, you can't have it because I'm on maternity leave"? There's a lot of pressure to do things. A lot of it probably comes from me, too, because I feel obligated to keep up on what my responsibilities were, but a lot of it was the corporation, which you can't control. That is, you have no control over your workload and your individual time. I mean, I have a lot of deadlines and things like that imposed on me that I just can't do anything about.

And another woman explained how she managed working and caring for her infant at the same time:

> I spent the first five weeks at home, and I had a computer terminal linked at home and an extra telephone. I spent the first five weeks at home with the baby in my arms typing on the computer terminal, talking on the phone—a little hectic.

Because some women may have specialized jobs or because co-workers may not have enough knowledge to cover specific issues or handle certain clients, women are often expected to continue managing these responsibilities from home. Pregnancy leaves are not, however, treated like other medical cases, such as heart attacks; the latter are construed as accidental and the former as intentional. The victim of a heart attack cannot be held responsible for illness, whereas women can be chastised, usually indirectly, for not "controlling" their biology. Continued work responsibility is a way to compensate for having a baby—perhaps because women feel so visible and exposed in their new roles as token females. Truly token in number (Kanter, 1977), they overcompensate as a way to demonstrate that they are just like men—loyal and committed.

Most career women openly acknowledge that they are being judged by their male co-workers and superiors, and they believe that their behavior about children will affect the attitudes of the men around them. One childless woman, who would like to stay home when her planned child is young, feels she cannot because

> I think feminism has a lot to do with my concern about having a child, and that's one of the things that I had wrestled with. I am thought of as likely to be the first woman in our firm who would be elected principal, and there isn't one now. . . . If I even have a child, then I've confirmed all sorts of stereotypes—"Oh my God, there's another one who just went out and had a kid after we've put all these years into her. How are we ever to have any women as principals if they all leave?"—and I may damage the opportunity for women who come behind me.

Another woman told how her short maternity leave eased the feelings of male bosses and set the corporate policy for managers' maternity leaves.

> When I found out I was pregnant, I then told my boss, and he was shattered, even though he knew that I was trying to get pregnant. You know, a "You're doing this to me" kind of reaction. "How am I going to tell the other guys on the block that I've got a pregnant manager?" He started out by informing me that I had the same amount of maternity leave policy as the secretaries, which is essentially that you don't get paid. You are promised a job of equivalent status if you return within approximately six months. I told him that was all very nice, and I told him I would call him.
>
> Now I was the first woman manager on corporate staff *at all.* And I was the first nonsecretarial person to get pregnant. This corporation had no experience and the maternity policy was written at that time. Two months after I got back, he got a call from the *Sun-Times,* which was doing a survey on the corporate experience with pregnancies. He informed them that this corporation really didn't think it was an issue. So he had done a political turnaround.

The strategy of waiting to have children until the wife has achieved a certain corporate position was the normative approach of these dual-career couples. One woman explained where she wants to be in her career in order to make the decision to have children:

> We are planning on having children in the next couple of years. The decision probably won't be made until we've determined it's time to do it. [Based on what?] To a great degree on where I end up in my career. I want to get to a certain point where I feel that I have achieved enough independence or stability or something career-wise to say, "Now I'm mature and financially affluent enough to take the next step."

The timing of children normally follows a promotion; one woman explained why: "I planned the pregnancy around my career cycle, my cycle between being promoted to principal and my next cycle to partner. This was a two-year period, where I could afford to have a little bit of slippage in my performance." Behind these strategies is the fear that those in power will feel that children create dual loyalties—to work and to family—for women, given the cultural expectation that women are primarily responsible for children. To avoid being denied promotions, women may time their pregnancies accordingly, as this example indicates:

> One woman, who is a senior officer, did something really wonderful. She announced that she was pregnant the day after they gave her the promotion to senior officer, and no one knew it. It wasn't like she was telling people as a public announcement, but she was telling the people who had made the decision—the board of directors.

However, there are always new career goals to achieve and higher corporate positions to strive for, and pursuing these aspirations can result in an indefinite postponement of children. One woman commented on the next career obstacle that must be crossed before she and her husband can have children:

> And that's probably why earlier I said I wouldn't start to think about having children for a year. Because right now I'm starting to manage my first study, and I want to get through having managed at least three before I think about that, because it's going to take a lot of energy to do the study and do it well so that people know you can do it.

Although not directly concerned with external organizational factors that may transform plans to have children into indefinite postponement, Veevers (1973) has argued that the prolonged postponement of a decision to have children is a major reason that marriages remain childless. The process of prolonged postponement, according to Veevers, "is one of recognizing an event which has already occurred, rather than of posing a question and then searching or negotiating for an answer" (344). With the biological clock ticking and decisions about children unresolved, many dual-career couples may end up childless. As one woman stated, "So here I am. I'm thirty-one, and I'm wondering if I am going to be fifty-two and still wondering if I'm going to have children."

Although the majority of childless couples expected to have children in the next couple of years, at each earlier juncture they had decided to wait.[2] These husbands and wives did volunteer a timeframe for having children, but they also expressed their reluctance to make a firm

2. Census data (U.S. Bureau of the Census, 1984, 2–3) reveal a significant decline between 1976 and 1982 in the percentage of childless women who expected to remain childless. In 1976, 68 percent of childless wives under the age of thirty expected to remain childless, but by 1982 only 53 percent expected to do so. The Census Bureau suggests that changes in the timing of childbearing during the late 1970s resulted in more women who actually desire children being temporarily childless.

decision. One man said, "We have talked about having children. The answer has always been, 'Children are something we ought to talk about someday.' "

With amniocentesis becoming a common medical procedure and articles in magazines featuring famous actresses and busy career women having their first children in their mid- to late thirties (see, for example, *Newsweek,* 1981a), women believe they now have an extended reprieve before the biological clock stops. Both medical and popular accounts feed into and perhaps legitimate the postponement process. As a result, when women pass the expected age for getting pregnant, they simply set a later age as the right time. For example, one woman commented that

> I used to say I was going to have a baby when I was thirty, and I just turned thirty last week. It wouldn't bother me right now to get pregnant, but I'm not taking my temperature or staying home or missing business trips because it is the day. . . . My husband's thirty-four, and we don't want to have kids that late in life. We don't want to be too old, but thirty used to be the magic number for women. I think it's now thirty-eight.

The experience of friends and older family members can sometimes provide a benchmark to establish the acceptability of having children in one's mid-thirties. One woman's reference group has helped expand the age norms for having children:

> When I did turn thirty-one this year, it was worse than turning thirty. Because what happened to me when I turned thirty didn't have anything to do with the whole thing about being up against the clock, the biological clock. It had more to do with the fact that now you're thirty—you're in your thirties, and so what you're accomplishing is what you ought

to be accomplishing. . . . So that was thirty. When I turned thirty-one, I wasn't doing the things that I expected to be doing by this time—things like having a family.

Most significant to me is that most of the women I know waited until they were thirty or thirty-one [to have children]. My cousins did that, and as I said, my sister's thirty-six and is thinking seriously about what she's going to do; most of my good friends from college, my best friends, don't have children. A number of them aren't married. But the women I know who are married waited until they were thirty, and a number of them are now thirty-four and having their first child. So what's happening to me is all those people are starting to have children. And so what happens to a lot of people maybe in their late twenties hasn't happened to me yet.

## DILEMMAS OF PARENTING AND CAREERS

For women in this study, the traditional female role has been expanded beyond being responsible for the home and children to include being an economic provider as well. Expectations about husbands' responsibilities have, however, remained virtually unaltered. Moreover, the expansion of the female role has not altered *how* traditional responsibilities are to be met. For these women, images of motherhood involve raising a child full-time as their own mothers did, not providing for children as their fathers did. Impressed indelibly in their minds are childhood memories of mother who was always there to serve milk and cookies after school, to act as chauffeur, to fix dinner, and to help with homework. This image is the yardstick against which men and women measure childrearing practices.

Even if women achieve equity with husbands through

participation in the work world, it does not necessarily follow that men achieve equity with women through parenting obligations. Men have yet to expand the static provider role of father into a fully active role of fathering. In part, women have not insisted that their husbands become actively involved in fatherhood. The adherence of career-oriented women to the masculine prototype has led both men and women alike to undermine the value of female qualities and responsibilities, such as nurturance and childrearing. Men, having failed to develop a fathering model, feel no desire to share mothering tasks. Therefore, childrearing activities remain the responsibility of wives, because women have always been subordinates of men. Even though a husband may not think of his own wife in this fashion, he thinks of other women in this way; and because his wife is a woman, *she* is expected to assume the major childrearing responsibilities.

This assumption poses a dilemma for career women; on the one hand, they are expected to meet traditional motherhood norms of "being there" while their child grows; on the other hand, their identity is based on what they do, a self-image derived from labor force participation and adherence to a masculine prototype. The dilemma of the work-mothering trade-off is typified by this childless woman's comments:

> [Having children] would be a big change in our lifestyle. I think that when kids are young, someone should stay home and look after them until they are ready for school. Neither my husband nor I are willing to stay home for five or six years. I just can't imagine *not* working. But I can't imagine my kids with someone else, either.
>
> Kids have become less important for me than they were three or four years ago. What is more important for me is to know that I can control my life and do that through

> working. If I had kids and dropped out of the job market for five years, I'm sure I would not be at the same level of my job. I would have dropped back some.

If women are to meet traditional motherhood obligations, they will have to leave the labor force and jeopardize the equality they have with their husbands. But if women are to retain their identity and symmetry with their husbands—something they have gained through employment—then they must alter their views on mothering. One woman stated:

> When we decided to have a kid, I decided I wanted to be a mom, a little bit, or why have a child? I just felt that if I am going to raise this kid, I want to be there for *some* of the events. Otherwise, I wouldn't have bothered.

This initial dilemma, faced prior to childbearing by every woman in this study, was resolved by altering the family organization to accommodate two careers and children, not by fundamentally reorganizing the work world or by directing a conscious set of demands against employers.

Men, especially those without children, did say they would like to assume a more active role in childrearing than their fathers had taken. One man, for example, thought that if his wife made enough money to support the family, he would like to give up his present career and its demands and pursue full-time writing, which is for him only a pastime now, combining this with raising a child. Other men wanted to spend their days in sports activities, which they felt could easily be combined with full-time childrearing. When men had other interests that they felt defined (or could in the future define) more fully who they were than could their paid employment, they thought about the possibility of remaining at home with a young infant while their wives continued in their own careers. Nevertheless, most men really did not think they would carry out these plans.

> I've teased her, although I do mean it half seriously, that if she becomes pregnant I'll quit my job, and I'll stay home and take care of the kid and write. I could see doing that. I mean, if it's anything like taking care of my cat, it's going to be a picnic. But I'm concerned that my earning power will remain higher than hers for some time. Economically, it is probably not feasible.

In most cases, however, men did not want to be full-time fathers. Role reversal is not a solution to problems of equality in marriage, because it places husbands in the same position that wives occupied in an earlier generation; nor is it necessarily a source of individual personal satisfaction. Most men have not developed (and probably do not foresee developing) alternative ways to assert their identities. Status and prestige are still derived from labor force participation, not from rearing children. Until childrearing is elevated to a status equal to that of paid employment, "real" contributions to society can only be made through paid employment. One man recounted what he thinks his children expect of him:

> I think it will make a lot of sense at that point [when he has achieved a particular corporate position and his child is four years old] for me to spend more time at home than I do now. I'll probably spend a hundred nights away from home this year, and I think I'd enjoy fathering and staying home more often. Full-time, at-home fathering I think is crazy, and I wouldn't do it. . . . If I were a kid and I found out that my father had held back his contribution to society really significantly because he was fathering, I'd be really angry. I mean, that's dumb.

Yet, ironically, women have always been denied the opportunity to make those same career contributions because of their responsibility for children. Women in earlier generations who lived vicariously through their husbands' and children's achievements initially did not know what to do with themselves when their children left home (Bart, 1972, 1975; Sheehy, 1977; Rubin, 1979); in some cases this event created psychological problems for these women.

But this set of problems is not a major focus in today's society, where being a full-time wife and mother is often portrayed as "not enough." The value attached to a college education for women has approached, if not surpassed, the value that has always applied to men's education. Husbands and wives expect each other to work for pay. In this regard, the women's movement has met one of its goals: "the problem that has no name," as Friedan (1963) called it, should no longer be a problem for the woman of the 1980s—middle-class women, or the women who did invisible work for corporations in the 1950s as wives of the "organization men," are no longer trapped in the home and can freely pursue careers that utilize their education (Rossi, 1964). Paid work has become a crucial source of women's identity, just as it is for men. Instead of deriving status from a husband's occupation, women may acquire independent status from their own occupations. Whereas a wife of "leisure" was once a sign that a husband was a successful breadwinner, the new wife of the 1980s should come equipped with her own career. Because these dual-career couples have established relationships based on respect for each other's careers, work outside the home is a necessary component of both the individual's life and the couple's marital relationship. Aware that work is central to many women's self-images, one woman argued that the issue is not employment itself but the independent identity that employment helps provide:

> I derive a lot of my self-image from work. It wouldn't *have* to be from work, because eighty years ago I would have derived my self-image from being a suffragette . . . or leading slaves to the underground. . . . I need more than just an immediate home life to derive my self-identity. But it doesn't necessarily have to be a work environment, though that's the environment I've chosen.

Because it is no longer assumed that women will remain at home, the problem now is how to have children and two careers simultaneously. When these couples begin to talk about having children, their attitudes about gender roles are brought to the surface. Remarkably, their discussions all come to the same conclusion: it is the wife who should decide to have or not to have children, as she is the one who has the most to lose in the workplace.

> My general answer, which I guess I believe, is that if Cindy wanted to have children, I would be delighted to be a parent. If Cindy doesn't want to have children, I would be delighted not to be a parent. Being a parent is not a drive in my life. I think I would be a good one. I don't care whether I am or not. On a scale of plus to minus on the issue, I am dead set at zero. And the other half is going to have to push me to a plus or minus. She has the most to lose, at least the nine months, so there would have to be some interest on her part before anything would ever happen.

In addition, discussions about how to rear children and who should be responsible for them tend to result in a traditional solution: women are charged with the responsibility for children. This man explained:

> I suppose that we both agree that . . . I am best suited for the role of the breadwinner and . . . to the extent that she

> accepts that and I accept that as given, there was really no option in terms of choices for me.
>
> I had no preference. . . . Essentially, in my view, it was her choice whether she wanted to stay at home with the baby or shift to a part-time career. . . . I don't have any strong feelings one way or the other. I'm not convinced that it will have any impact on the development of the child either way, so essentially I felt it was her decision. She chose, for a number of reasons, I think, to continue with her career.

During these discussions the wife's financial worth is evaluated, especially in cases where couples pool their money. When the wife's salary is not commensurate with her husband's—that is, when he makes $40,000 and she makes $30,000—her lesser earnings are used to legitimate his role as primary breadwinner. Children are not seen as a "cost" or a "tax" of his earnings and, therefore, having children should not alter his career in any way. Although the husband may be aware that his wife is discriminated against in the workplace because of her sex, he in effect further discriminates against her by using her lower salary as a basis for determining (and legitimating) her career sacrifices.

> We both wanted a family—two kids—and when the kids entered the picture it obviously became more difficult to keep all these things in the air—two kids and two careers. Our decision was to run to the more traditional, where my wife would have the major responsibility for the direction of the kids until they were in school. As a result she is limping along in terms of her career. We talked about it. But I have personally never seriously considered severing my career, at any stage, to stay home with the kids like Janet would. However, if the compensation had been equal, maybe I would have considered it, because I don't

see my skills becoming less sharp or obscure if I laid out for a few years. Janet thinks hers will because of the high technology in her industry. But we can't live on her income, and she's not paid what I think she is worth.

Not only is present salary assessed but future earnings and career advancement also are considered by couples. As one woman stated, "It only made sense that my career should be the one to suffer. Even though we make the same now, it is an artifact. My husband has greater future earning potential than I do." In other words, differences in earnings and earning power can do what "liberated" men and women refuse to do: force women to assume traditional responsibility for children. But the converse can also be true. In those rare cases where the wife earns more than her husband, he may be the one to have more daily childcare responsibility. One couple determined that the wife would make more money and advance in her career faster than the husband. Fed up with the corporate rat race, he wanted to become involved in childrearing.

> I am the one who has primary responsibility for our child. My wife travels a lot, and I'm there every day to relieve the sitter. I would say that, if push came to shove, I would probably stay home in an emergency. If I didn't like our childcare arrangements, I would immediately quit work and stay home.

Another male without children commented, "Since I make much less than my wife, if one of us had to stay home with the children, it would be me." In the overwhelming majority of cases, the couples' discussions revolve around the role of the wife within the family. Is she to take on full-time motherhood and give up her career, or will couples instead alter their perceptions about mothering to accommodate the wife's career?

Similar strategies for integrating children into their lives were outlined by couples with and without children.[3] The relative emphasis couples place on parenting, as opposed to careers, determines the strategy they choose: (1) adhering to a masculine prototype both in the family and the work realm, (2) decreasing job demands in exchange for small doses of mothering, (3) downgrading the importance of careers so that the woman can devote more time to mothering, or (4) leaving the labor force for full-time mothering. These strategies all require either a redefinition of norms for motherhood or an alteration of job and career plans.

### *Masculine Prototype*

Stringent adherence to masculine patterns for career success most commonly relegates family concerns and children to the background. Couples who choose this strategy try to ensure that family obligations do not impede the wife's career. One woman described the goals she had at the time of her child's birth: "One was to be back at work two weeks after my child was born, and the other was to run a marathon shortly after. I met both my goals."

Women choose to resume their careers as soon as possible after childbirth in order to demonstrate their "man-

3. Daniels and Weingarten (1982), in a study that included women from a wide variety of jobs, found two patterns for combining motherhood and work outside the home. These patterns applied both to women who had their children as young adults and to those who had their children in their late twenties and early thirties. Daniels and Weingarten found that timing makes a difference in whether women followed a sequential or a simultaneous pattern of combining work and family. Women who had children later were fairly evenly divided between the two patterns, whereas those who had their children earlier were eight times as likely to have opted for a sequential pattern.

hood." Like the first generation of kibbutz women who were allowed to work in the fields alongside men (Talmon, 1972; Blumberg, 1977), these women follow the masculine prototype to confirm their equal status, because they are in highly visible positions. Women's behavior is purposive because they are fighting for equal footing with their male co-workers. In the competitive work environment, an important "rite of passage" for females is their response to the issue of motherhood. They meet this test of their "manhood" by finding surrogates to care for their children, and they become, like their husbands, economic providers. The same pattern of work and travel continues after the birth of a child. One woman recounted her child's reaction to her late hours at the office and her frequent overnight business trips: "With my son, my husband says that when I am not home Johnny sleeps through the night. When I'm home, he's determined to guarantee himself some time with me. So he gets up between 2 and 5 A.M."

### *Trimming Work Demands*

Another strategy is to reduce job demands where possible, such as decreasing the optional long hours spent working late in the office or the time spent socializing after hours with co-workers. Unlike women who fit children into their schedules, some women plan their work schedules around the care of their children. They commonly rise long before children awake to finish the prior day's work instead of working longer hours at night in the office. One woman, who lives two blocks from her office, told me that she does go into work on Saturdays, and related how she scheduled that work time: "I will come in on a Saturday, when my daughter is napping. I can get a lot more done in one hour on Saturday than working three hours on Friday, because I don't get disturbed." Rearranging work time enables these women to devote time to mothering. One woman contrasted her work style before and after the birth of her child, illustrating the effect children had on her work:

> It's a tough situation. I would say our lives were really easy before we had the baby. If I wanted to work until ten o'clock, it was no big deal. But it's a lot more complicated with the baby, and I'm the one bearing the burden of it, not that I think it's unfair. I mean, I really love getting up with the baby and being home with the baby early at night. So my work suffers.

When women feel they cannot ignore the informal demands of paid work or when travel cannot be negotiated with bosses, they change jobs—but do not relinquish their careers—to regularize their work schedule, as did this mother:

> I gave up traveling when I had my first child. The other alternative would have been to have a live-in babysitter, and neither of us really wanted to go that route. And I just really wanted more time to be with my children. I mean, when I decided to have children, it was with the decision that I would try to have more time with them and a somewhat regular life in terms of my professional commitment. I found a job that didn't demand that I travel. So I try very hard to have breakfast with them in the morning, then go to work, and come home—leave the office promptly at five o'clock.

Other women, especially those with professional degrees, spoke of establishing their own businesses or looking for less demanding work in their fields. This plan was described by one woman who had no children:

> When you work for a firm like this, you have to turn out what everybody else turns out. You have to leave when everybody else leaves, and sometimes things do come up when you have to work late. I might leave here and get a job, like down in Hyde Park. The American Bar Foundation is down there, the University of Chicago is down there. So, it may be possible for me to do that—to work closer to home. Even to work full-time and be closer to home and within walking distance would knock two hours off your day away from the kid, and that would be good. But I know that I would have to take a cut in pay.

Another woman remained in her dead-end job, postponing a career-enhancing move because the new job would have meant commuting too far from her home. Strategies such as these hinge on routinizing hours and decreasing travel—both commuting time and trips out of town. As Blumberg (1977) points out in her study of working women around the world, the more compatible with childrearing the essential productive work of a society is, the higher status and the more power women have in that society. The ideology of mothering is not totally relinquished, but its practice as a daily full-time occupation is.

### *Part-Time Jobs and Full-Time Mothering*

The third strategy women in dual-career couples follow is to individually negotiate a part-time or three-quarter-time work arrangement with bosses.[4] These women work either three or four days in the office and stay at home the remaining days, although they report that they con-

4. Only three women in this study tried this strategy. The majority of women were more likely to try a combination of the first two strategies.

tinue to do office work at home on their days "off." In effect, they receive part-time pay for full-time work. Nevertheless, these women are grateful to be allowed to work in this arrangement, and in some instances they become even more committed to their employers. Because they officially work part-time, however, they are treated as second-class citizens and accorded minimal authority. Their commitment to their careers and employers is often questioned. One woman described what she gave up for this kind of work arrangement:

> When my child was born, I was thirty-three years old, and I was in a position where I was a boss. I could no longer be a boss part-time, and it's hard to give up authority—that has been the hardest thing for me. My position just wasn't five days, nine to five. There was lots of travel, lots of nights, lots of weekends. So I made the decision when I got pregnant to see about working part-time.

However, although an individual boss or corporation may be willing to make such an arrangement, these plans do not always work out:

> When I first went back to work after my child was born, I went back four days a week. After a year of that, it was just clear that it wasn't working out from either one of our perspectives. Things always happened on the day I was not going to be in the office. There was something that had to be done, and it's hard to say to a client that I'm not going to be able to finish their project tomorrow because tomorrow's my day off. It just didn't work out, and so finally I went back to five days.

This woman chose to return to full-time employment. However, it is also possible that her choice might have been to leave paid work altogether, the fourth strategy available to women. This strategy was not chosen by anyone in this study, but those women (and their spouses) who feel that childrearing is best done only by the biological mother will decide to leave the labor force.

Any ambivalence that women in this sample felt about not remaining home full-time with their children was dispelled during maternity leaves. During this time the importance of paid work is challenged: when cut off from the world of work, a woman's identity is threatened. One woman described what she learned about herself shortly after her first child was born:

> I took three weeks off with my first child, and it was at that point that I was climbing walls. . . . My husband came home one night and the two of us, the baby and I, were sitting there crying and obviously had been for some time. He proceeded to put us in separate rooms, settle her down first, and then settle me down, and call the sitter and ask her if she could start full-time the next day. He just announced that I was going back to work the next day whether I wanted to or not, because he really couldn't afford the psychiatrist bills.
>
> I wasn't prepared. I did not know what having a child was going to be like, and when I found out what it was like, I didn't want any part of it. So I went back after three weeks. I need the work environment at least for part of the day. I went back part-time at first.

Another woman's husband, although initially less supportive, did not admit the importance of a career for his wife until their first child was born. Over the years he had managed to assure himself that his was the primary career (they made identical salaries) and that motherhood would eventually fulfill his wife.

> She didn't realize how stultifying an environment it would be for her to have a career and yet not be working, even in the short time when she didn't work after giving birth. I admit also that I was not all that supportive, as I thought I would surely be. I thought, "How in the hell can you com-

plain about being home all day when all you have to do is watch a little kid sleep in the bassinet?"

I had no idea that my wife's career was important to her, because I had convinced myself that what she did was relatively unimportant, although it was nice to have the income. I didn't see her career as being one of the great contributions to life. That's my narrow-mindedness, I recognize, but I figured she would have no problems with staying at home, and at some time she would go back to work, but there was no rush. Now I see that it is indispensable for her that she work, and frankly, I think her working will probably be indispensable in our marriage forever.

In all cases women were the ones to take maternity leaves, not their husbands. Staying home for the first time (even for only a couple of months) challenges the established symmetrical relationship between husbands and wives, where equality was assumed because both partners were involved in identical activities. Who worked outside the home did not hinge on gender, and neither partner remained at home. Yet gender becomes a salient issue once children arrive: someone has to be with them. Women are still viewed by these couples as better equipped to nurture young children, even though their lives until this point have paralleled those of their male peers and husbands. These women have learned to measure their worth against the work world, by credentials, degrees, promotions, and salaries. This world has provided their reference group, and many have unlearned stereotypical female traits and adopted male behaviors in their place. But staying home, even for a maternity leave, is a reminder that they are different. And as a result, instead of viewing the bond between mother and child as unique (the mainstream attitude of two decades ago) or female nurturance as positive, they view it as unfair. Because infants unilaterally affect the work lives of women only, some women resent husbands who go off to work while they remain at home. One woman expressed these sentiments pointedly:

> I really love going home to my baby and that kind of thing, but I was crazy by the end of the four weeks. I felt cut off from the world. There was nobody to talk to during the day, and I needed to come back to work. I began to really resent my husband going out to work. My credentials are as good if not better than his, and he's the one going out to work and I'm sitting here changing diapers, and I felt kind of silly.

Therefore, it is often during a woman's maternity leave that the couple realizes just how crucial paid work is to the wife's identity (and perhaps to their marriage as well). Many of these women simply cannot adjust to full-time motherhood. Whether their identification with a career explains why they went back to work or whether it is a justification for a commitment to return to work made prior to having children cannot be determined from these interviews. One point is clear, however, and will be explored in the next chapter: these women went back to working outside the home and committed themselves to a system in which a surrogate released them to pursue their careers.

# 5
# CHILDCARE ARRANGEMENTS: Helping Hands

HOW ARE CHILDREN to be cared for? Although the range of possible childcare alternatives is relatively large—paid or unpaid relatives, communally organized childcare, or organizationally provided childcare—the majority of dual-career couples in this study chose to fulfill their childcare needs in a much more individualized fashion, namely, hiring individual babysitters or housekeepers. Given the multiple demands on husbands' and wives' time arising from their individual careers, it is not surprising that childcare should necessarily involve the inclusion of a third party. Two central questions are raised by this finding: first, why the hired labor alternative is the most common childcare arrangement for these couples; and second, how the introduction of a market exchange (between service seller and service buyer) is squared with the traditional norms of nonmarket exchange within the family. These two questions will be explored in this chapter, along with the implications of childcare practices for gender roles in the family.

## HIRED LABOR VERSUS ALTERNATIVE APPROACHES

For couples who have decided to have children but who have also decided that having children will not terminate either spouse's career, childcare arrangements are usually planned in light of both functional necessity and normative considerations. At a minimum, the routine availability of a childcare person or facility during the days of the workweek is required; but this need can also extend to evenings or weekends, when work demands may take priority. To meet the needs of the dual-career couple, the childcare worker or organization must therefore be available on a continuous or on-demand basis and must supply a relatively predictable quality of care. Childcare arrangements must also be affordable, as the cost of childcare is a substantial expense in the couple's budget.

Although the functional aspects of childcare arrangements are important, normative concerns also exist and may occasionally crosscut functional necessity. Traditional norms of childrearing in general and of mothering in particular act to discourage a purely consumer mentality about procuring childcare services. As is the case with schools, parents expect institutions that provide care not only to educate and supervise children in their absence but also to supply an additional element of concern, caring, and guidance for children. It is even more commonly expected that parents should seek to provide an environment of caring and nurturance for their children when the children are least able to act autonomously. Although some dispute remains about the effect of children's social environment on their social and psychological development, most parents consider a close association between themselves and their children to be important. Most Western societies have traditionally emphasized the close bond between natural parents—especially mothers—and children. When such bonds and expectations are at least partially violated by the demands of two careers, the nature and quality of alternate childcare gains increased importance as a surrogate for the close parent-child or mother-child relationship. Hence, although a strategy for career enhancement might suggest childcare arrangements that are most practical and most easily accommodate career demands, the norms of parenting and childrearing lead parents to desire the highest quality childcare available.

Given these general considerations, what are the alternatives for childcare? Two broad dimensions can be used to categorize childcare alternatives: (1) whether care is provided by an individual or by an organization, and (2) whether the nature of the relationship between the service provider and service consumer is marketized or nonmarketized. The various combinations of these two dimensions result in four sets of alternatives (see the accompanying figure). In this sample the majority of couples with children fell into quadrant A: they hire childcare workers on an individual basis. Why is that op-

Dimensions of Childcare Alternatives

| | *Individualized* | *Organized* |
|---|---|---|
| *Marketized* | A<br>Hired labor | B<br>Commercial |
| *Nonmarketized* | C<br>Family, friends | D<br>Publicly sponsored, parent- or company-sponsored |

tion the most common? Part of the explanation lies in the lack of real alternatives. But equally important, the lack of alternatives itself results from a lack of demand by couples needing childcare service. On the one hand, arrangements such as company-sponsored childcare are so rarely available that they are not really viable alternatives;[1] but, on the other hand, the nonexistent or as yet ineffective demands by employees for such services also help to explain why organization-sponsored childcare is not common. Before considering the popularity of the hired labor option (and the problems it presents), it is useful to consider why other childcare alternatives are less frequently pursued.

## *Family and Close Friends*

If one starts with the assumption that couples seek to maximize the quality of childcare while minimizing its cost, then it seems reasonable that they would use family or close friends as a childcare option.[2] From a tradi-

1. According to former U.S. Secretary of Health and Human Services Margaret Heckler, the number of employers offering childcare services increased 289 percent from 1979 to 1983, from 200 to 600 employers in the nation. Ninety-eight percent of all the companies in the United States have no childcare policy at all (Berstein, 1983).

2. After examining the research on the kinds of arrangements used by mothers to care for their children from the late 1960s to 1980, Floge (1985) draws these general conclusions: "In all of the studies, care by relatives was found to account for a major share of all daycare used—anywhere from 40 percent to 80 percent, depending on the group considered and the measurement used. Group daycare centers, on the other hand, provided only a small proportion of the childcare, usually under 15 percent" (144).

My study supports the general finding of other research that a woman's occupation is related to the kind of childcare she uses. Angrist et al. (1976) found that blue-collar and service workers used care by relatives more often than paid care, whereas professional and managerial workers used paid care more frequently than any other occupational group.

tional viewpoint, extended family members—such as grandmothers, mothers-in-law, sisters, aunts, or nieces—could provide the optimal arrangement. Family ties and shared beliefs about childrearing suggest a measure of agreement and predictability regarding the conditions of care, and these family members have a vested interest in the child. Furthermore, the cost of this care might be relatively low or might even be exchanged for other services. Hence, both the functional and normative requirements of childcare could be fulfilled within an environment that more closely approximates family arrangements than does any other option.

But there are numerous factors mitigating against the viability of this option. For many dual-career couples, the location of their worksite takes them away from close networks of extended kin; career demands may require leaving the neighborhood and often the city where their family resides. Also, the reduced importance of extended family ties—caused by physical separation or by long periods spent away from family during college and graduate work—has diminished the possibility that significant demands can be made on family members for childcare. In addition, families are expected to be self-sufficient, and this expectation reduces reliance on extended family ties. Many couples believe that their income is or ought to be sufficient to enable them to arrange childcare without incurring financial or, more important, familial indebtedness. Finally, postponing children often means that grandparents are too old to be eager to care for children. Although extended kin may be used as an occasional fallback option (for an emergency or to meet an unanticipated demand), these instances tend to be the exception rather than the rule, and, in most cases, family-based childcare is neither a viable nor a routine option.

### *Commercial Childcare*

Childcare options are not limited to individualized arrangements, however. The two principal alternatives to family and hired labor are commercially and communally organized group childcare arrangements. Commercial childcare facilities have mushroomed, particularly as the number of married women in the labor force has increased. Commercial childcare enterprises, in the form of either small units (such as individually licensed homes) or larger, even franchised operations, have the advantage of providing services tailored to the needs of working parents; they usually open early in the morning and often remain open until the early evening. Most such establishments must be certified by public agencies, and this offers some measure of assurance that certain standards of child supervision, protection, and, perhaps, education and nutrition are being met.

Although the services provided by commercial enterprises tend to satisfy the functional requirements of childcare, they often fail or are perceived to fail in the area of normative requirements for quality. When she investigated commercial daycare enterprises, one woman found that "there is no full-time daycare to take kids as young as John [age two] that I have yet located in this area. Well, maybe there are some, but not of the quality I would want." Given the large number of children often supervised in commercial operations, many couples suspect that the quality of care is reduced by the enterprise's desire to maximize the efficiency of its operations and thereby maximize its profits. Parents sometimes suggest that the quality of care their children receive in a franchised daycare operation resembles the quality of product one receives from a fast-food franchise. After being in a business environment, these couples are all too familiar with the imperatives of profitability. More commonly, it is suggested that, although commercial childcare may be all right for other families, a higher quality of care is desirable for those who can afford it. This man's response captures the sentiments of these couples about daycare:

> For some couples who don't have financial resources available, daycare is probably the way to go. But no way are we going to go through that. I know it is not for me; it's not for my son. . . . I have a more traditional view. I just think it is nicer for my child to be at home. I get turned off when I see the little cots lined up and stuff like that. I think it's kind of depressing, but that's me.

Couples seek an arrangement in which quality of care more closely approximates that of the traditional family; they equate quality with intensity and one-on-one care, believing this to be the best substitute for the traditional mother. This mother explained her choice to hire a daytime, in-home childcare provider and revealed a number of unfounded stereotypical fears about other types of group childcare:

> At that time [seven years ago] $70 a week was expensive to pay someone to come into my home and care for my child. I could have taken him to somebody else's house for about $30 a week but I was willing to pay a $40 premium just to know that he had a one-on-one relationship and he wasn't in a group of other kids where he'd get taken care of on a rotation basis. I wanted him at home in familiar surroundings, because that way he'd feel secure. I think a lot of children do end up out of the home, and particularly when the woman is taking care of more than one other child, you find certain levels of anxiety in the children and they're less secure.

For these parents, certification of an organization does not provide sufficient reassurance that the child will be individually supervised, and, as their income is adequate, they do not hesitate to make alternative childcare arrangements.

### *Group Childcare*

Communally organized group childcare is another option. As noted in the figure (p. 149), there are at least three possible arrangements: publicly sponsored, company-sponsored, and parent-sponsored childcare. Although four children were in nursery school for part of the day in addition to being cared for by a housekeeper, none of the couples interviewed in this study used these group childcare options exclusively.[3] For example, one husband speculated on childcare options he would prefer when he and his wife had a child:

> I think it would be great if they would have an expensive childcare center located downtown in the Loop here someplace. High price, but maybe a lot of people would be willing to have that available. We don't have a solution yet, and in a sense we're hanging back and saying, "Let's see what happens."

He would be willing to pay the high costs that he considers indicative of quality in order to ensure a certain exclusivity of the facility.

3. Steinberg and Green (1979), focusing on the reasons parents choose particular childcare options, found that many people consider convenience important. Reliability and continuity of care were also critical, as Lein's (1979) research shows. Even though the couples cited in this chapter did not choose group childcare exclusively, it was sometimes used in combination with housekeepers for part of the day. Parents felt that employing housekeepers best ensured continuity and reliability; additionally, children were often also enrolled in programs such as nursery school to provide a social environment with other children. Lein states that parents will choose such multiple-care arrangements in order to meet several conflicting priorities.

Examining why these group options are so infrequently chosen leads to further insight into the social organization of the dual-career family. Each group childcare option has the advantage of being organized to meet the needs of working couples with children. Furthermore, all are less likely than commercial childcare to be influenced by the objective of profit making to the detriment of service delivery (for example, cost cutting, routinization of service, and an emphasis on efficiency over quality care). These childcare options can be placed on a continuum in terms of their responsiveness to the desires of their clientele. The standards of service delivery in publicly sponsored childcare are less likely to be affected by profit considerations than in commercial establishments and are more likely to reflect a concern for equal access to a social good. Like all social programs, however, publicly sponsored childcare might suffer from a tendency toward bureaucratization; standards of quality would be less affected by efficiency considerations, but rules about the provision of a social service might diminish responsiveness to the particular needs of segments of a diverse clientele.

Company-sponsored childcare might be more sensitive to the needs of parents and children, especially since such a service would be an employment-related benefit similar to salary and medical benefits and as such an inducement to stable work performance. Moreover, company-sponsored childcare is more easily tailored to the job situations of dual-career couples than either publicly or commercially provided childcare. Finally, communally organized group childcare, based on the cooperative efforts of parents with similar jobs and family situations, brings together people with similar needs and childrearing concerns. Cooperative arrangements of this sort could operate on a time-sharing basis, where each parent is committed to a set time span with a group of children. (An obvious drawback is that this arrangement requires a time commitment—possibly a sizeable one—from parents.) These parental childcare workers with a vested interest in the communal care of their children replace the hired labor found in commercial establishments or the government employees found in publicly sponsored childcare groups.

Several factors explain why group childcare options, despite their potential advantages, are infrequently used by dual-career couples. First, there are few examples of publicly or company-sponsored childcare. None of the couples interviewed reported that their employers had a childcare service. Several suggested that if such services were available, they would use them, but none reported any organized effort by company employees to request such a service. Although publicly sponsored childcare is more available, it is regarded less highly by these couples. Like commercial childcare, publicly sponsored care is considered acceptable for other families (particularly those whose incomes limit their choices) but not acceptable for those with incomes sufficient to allow a choice. One woman described her aversion to daycare:

> I am not a daycare fan at all. I have real bad feelings about it. It's almost like—oh my God, people wouldn't believe I support the ERA—it's almost like those kids are just abandoned. Abandoned—maybe that's too strong a word, but that's how I feel about the daycare thing. They take their kids there with fevers, they take them there with this and that. Why? Why get the kid sicker? Now, if you need the money and you're starving or you haven't got a husband, well that's different—that's a need. But I swear I've seen some of those kids—I know a couple of them, maybe three—they are a little lost.

If couples make too much money, the eligibility requirements for existing publicly sponsored childcare programs may also preclude this option. Perhaps because of their inability to qualify for these programs, some of the couples interviewed put publicly provided childcare in the same category as welfare. These couples do not consider it the government's responsibility to make childcare available to them, and they simply refrain from making claims for an equivalent service based on their rights as citizens.

Communally organized group childcare arrangements are the least frequently considered alternative, even though they would seem to offer the most advantages. The single most important obstacle to this option is the substantial time commitment demanded by individual careers. It is not inconceivable that a group of concerned parents could arrange a system of released time from work in order to participate in cooperative childcare, a pattern that may run counter to the usual expectations about work schedule but need not mean that work time is reduced. Rather, a portion of a given workday could be traded for childcare time and made up in the evening or on the weekend. Such a system is in fact more common for people in jobs where work schedules are less flexible—waitresses, nurses, or clerical workers, for example. But this option may seem very unconventional for dual-career couples, who tend to challenge the rules of the organization only infrequently.

Two additional factors—career and status—directly affect the choice of childcare alternatives and help to explain the popularity of the hired labor alternative. Career requirements, in terms of both time commitment and orientation toward work, clearly affect the childcare choice. Time commitments, particularly those associated with travel and extensive work-related socializing, limit the time individuals or couples can offer to innovative, and especially cooperative, childcare arrangements. In addition, the structure of careers—especially management-level positions—leads individuals to focus on highly particularistic goals. Careers and organizations are set up so that individual performance and evaluation are far more important for advancement than any group contribution. Individuals are routinely advised that advancement is brought about by "team" contributions to the organization, but most learn very quickly that a significant, if not more important, criterion for advancement is outstanding individual performance. The effect of such an emphasis is that individual performance is valued as the means to individual reward, and the virtues of collective effort are ignored or devalued. Given such an environment, collective action (even for goals shared by people in similar situations) is avoided in favor of individual action or individual solutions. Thus, even though people employed by the same organization may have similar situations or needs, they rarely consider collective claims against the organization as a viable alternative.

Status, or claims to status based on income, further encourages individual solutions. Many couples feel that they make enough money to enable them to purchase a service, rather than relying on solutions such as asking favors of family members. This drive for self-sufficiency is often fueled by a desire to be independent of family resources, particularly if these individuals had depended on those resources for their education. In some cases, the desire for self-sufficiency is combined with a drive by career women to retain a degree of the independence that led them to seek their own careers in the first place. Hence, needs for individual and family self-sufficiency are directly connected. Finally, the drive for self-sufficiency is also directly related to the couples' expectation that their lifestyle should reflect their income. These couples voice dissatisfaction with or outright disdain for publicly organized childcare, and they see these sentiments as appropriate for people of their economic and social position. Thus, although it would appear that a higher level of income and the development of two careers might open a greater range of childcare alternatives for these couples, in reality, their choices are highly constricted by the demands of careers and the status associated with them.

### *The Hired Labor Option*

Hiring an individual worker (herein referred to as the "hired labor option") is the most common form of childcare used by dual-career couples. This option offers the least troublesome solution to the problem of releasing women to pursue careers and is often chosen because other alternatives seem difficult or even impossible. But the hired labor alternative is itself paradoxical. On the one hand, it presents its own problems of maintenance and control—for example, how to demarketize a wage relationship for purposes of control. On the other hand, it is a system predicated on the availability of a disadvantaged class of laborers—at a general level, career opportunities are created for some women through the denial of those opportunities to other women. This point was made earlier by Hunt and Hunt (1977) and will be considered here in connection with the hired labor option, the paradox of trust in and control over childcare workers, and the "replacement" function of these workers.

## THE CONTRADICTIONS OF USING CHILDCARE PROVIDERS

The selection of a hired childcare worker realistically belongs to a class of decisions that includes the choice of a surgeon to perform major surgery, a chief accountant to handle one's business finances, or a lawyer to represent one in criminal proceedings. To most people, particularly those who do not have to face the choice, the dilemma of selecting a childcare worker might seem relatively minor and will certainly not seem as important as choosing who will perform an operation or prepare a legal defense. Yet, if one considers what a childcare worker is actually called on to do, the significance of the assignment—and therefore the choice—is much greater. In most situations, the worker is expected to supervise, care for, feed, protect, and guide a highly vulnerable and impressionable human being in the absence of the parents. As parents often declare that their children are their most precious possessions, the person or persons in whom they invest responsibility for the children must be skilled, responsible, responsive, and, perhaps most important, trustworthy. After all, many of these children spend over half their waking day in the company of this stranger. Nevertheless, childcare labor tends to be drawn from a pool of workers whose social and economic backgrounds differ considerably from those of their employers. These workers are expected to be satisfied with relatively low wages, as compared to the fees paid to other service providers (such as doctors, accountants, or lawyers) for equally critical services.

In analyzing the problems and practices of the hired labor option, three sets of questions must be considered. First, how do couples acquire such seemingly valuable labor at so low a price? In particular, how do they recruit and select potential childcare workers? Why are certain labor pools more attractive than others? And who is finally hired? Second, how do couples control that labor? How do they ensure that childcare workers perform their critical assignments reliably and conform to the couple's needs? Third, what effect does the employment of the individual childcare worker have on family roles and family organization?

### *Hired Help: Who Is the Most Attractive Labor Source?*

Ideally, the most attractive employee is the worker who is best trained and whose social background and values are most like those of the parents—someone who shares similar beliefs about childrearing practices, or who can be expected to submit, without question, to parents' views, and someone who will offer a measure of agreement, support, and, most important, trust and predictability to the parent–childcare worker relationship. A traditional governess or nanny would seem most desirable. Although the median income of these couples is relatively high, however, few can be considered (or consider themselves) wealthy enough to afford such a maidservant. Instead, they seek laborers who can be trained in childcare, who can be engaged in a continuous relationship, and who will be trustworthy and predictable, but who cannot effectively transform their skills and qualities into the high wage demands of a marketable profession.

Historically, racial and ethnic minorities have been sources of childcare labor. For example, black women have long been sought after as childcare workers, especially in smaller cities and towns. In the South, both before and after the Civil War, they were commonly employed to care for the children of white families. Reputational networks were used to select and ensure the acceptability of particular women. Given their generally disadvantaged status and their highly restricted employment opportunities, black women could be hired to perform important and sensitive chores in white families' homes without being able to demand wages commensurate with their skills. In other parts of the country, particularly during the first half of the twentieth century, young immigrant women were employed in a similar manner. These women were highly desirable workers because they did not have local kinship ties of their own that could foster dual loyalties. For many of these women, the employing family served as a protector against a world quite foreign to them. At the same time, however, the insular character of employment in a private household made them subject to nonmarket influences over the labor contract. For example, they could be required to work longer hours and accept greater restrictions on their freedom than most employers could demand in the open economy.

In the 1980s dual-career couples tend to employ childcare workers drawn from three principal sources: women under twenty-five, older women, and recent (legal or illegal) female immigrants. These women, compared to other labor market participants, are attractive as childcare workers because they generally have fewer skills and, more important, fewer employment opportunities than do men or citizens. They thus prove more adaptable to the particular demands made by dual-career couples, although, as this study will show, age, marital status, and immigration status have important effects on the kind of employment relationships these women develop with dual-career couples.

The particular childcare arrangement developed is determined, in part, by the relative importance couples attach to factors such as the cost of childcare, the flexibility of the individual childcare worker, and similarities in status or values of the worker. For example, when the cost of childcare is deemed most important, the differences in social background between the couple and a foreign childcare worker may be set aside in favor of the low relative cost of an undocumented immigrant worker. Or a couple may pay more or go out of their way to develop an arrangement with an older woman citizen so that someone of like background and values will care for their child. Decisions about the nature of the childcare arrangement—whether the worker will live in or commute daily and whether childcare will be located in the couple's home—help explain how and why couples hire from different segments of these distinctive labor pools.

Before examining how couples' demands affect the kinds of workers they hire, it is instructive to look more closely at the particular segments of the childcare labor force. Although this study was not designed to yield a representative sample of childcare workers, certain tentative conclusions about the composition of this labor force can be drawn from the interviews with dual-career families. Of the twenty-nine childcare workers represented in the interviews (including both current and past employees), 21 percent were young women under age twenty-five (including teenagers), 48 percent were older women, and 31 percent were immigrants (see Table 10).[4] The category of women under twenty-five includes teenage help from neighboring midwestern

4. I have not included in this total workers who left after only a few weeks, because the couples could remember very little about them.

TABLE 10. Type of Childcare Arrangement

| *Category of Worker* | *Live-In* | *Day Only* | *Percentage of Total Instances* |
|---|---|---|---|
| Teenagers and young women | 33% | 15% | 21% (6) |
| Older women | 22% | 60% | 48% (14) |
| Immigrant women | 44% | 25% | 31% (9) |
| Total | 99% (9) | 100% (20) | 100% (29) |

NOTE: N = 29. Figures rounded to the nearest percent.

states and help from young women whose lives were in transition. Childcare work is normally temporary. Teenagers may take these positions to get away from their own parents, as one woman commented when describing the background of her teenage help: "She never had a good relationship with her own parents, and she ran away when she was seventeen and lived with a man. She had all sorts of problems resulting from that, and so she was pretty screwed up."

Other young women may be either waiting for husbands to graduate from school or unable to afford care for their own child. Needing the money, they may resort to caring for another child in addition to their own. Another woman explained why childcare work was an interim job for the young woman she once employed:

> We could see, in terms of the ancillary duties, that she did not want to be doing childcare anymore. Finally, my husband talked to her husband, and what the story was, was that she wanted to go back to work. Not only did she not want to stay

> home with my child, she didn't particularly want to stay home with her child anymore, either.

Older women are the largest category of childcare workers. The class position of these women has either taken a downward turn or is in transition. Family income may be insufficient to support this disadvantaged group, so they turn to childcare work to supplement the income. The majority of these women are married, with teenagers or grown children of their own. One woman explained why her sitter continued taking care of her child even after the income was no longer needed:

> The school happened to know a lady who might take children for lunch and after school. She and her husband needed the money at the time. Now, Martha just does it as a favor because her husband's getting wealthier and wealthier.

Most of these women had once been full-time wives and mothers. Lacking alternative job skills, they turned to childcare. Couples whose housekeepers or sitters had reared children of their own were quick to point this out, perhaps because such experience is viewed as an informal certification for the job. For some childcare workers, the job allowed them to earn some money while still caring for their own children.

In general, instead of hiring a single worker for many years, couples in this sample hired a series of workers.[5] Most couples have had a combination of foreign and American domestics; the number of childcare workers an individual couple has employed is highly variable. For example, during a three-year period, the number of workers per couple ranged from one to nine women. Put

5. Emlen et al. (1974), sampling childcare providers, found that three-quarters of the arrangements were terminated within six months. About one-third of the arrangements were terminated by the childcare provider.

another way, twenty-nine childcare workers in all had been employed by the eleven couples with children.[6]

Once couples decide to employ an individual to care for their children, the actual arrangement of the childcare becomes an issue. This arrangement is not easily developed, nor is it necessarily permanent. The couple's own preferences regarding cost, accessibility, and the background of the childcare worker influence who gets hired and how and where the child is cared for. For many couples, their backgrounds initially argued against including an outsider, a nonfamily member, in the privacy of their home; with few exceptions, these dual-career couples do not have family histories that included experiences with hired childcare workers. Against her husband's wishes, one woman resisted live-in help with her first child:

> We wanted somebody to care for the child during the day. We had a large house, but I come from a very lower-middle-class background, and I am not used to help of any sort. The thought of anybody else living in my house was almost frightening. It was a total invasion of privacy. So my husband and I had a fight. He thought the only rational thing to do was to have live-in help but realized that I was not about to deal with this.

Only three couples initially hired live-in help, and they all reported having had solid middle-class upbringings. Several other couples eventually shifted to live-in help as they became more comfortable with their new class position. However, more than two-thirds of the childcare providers were day workers. Daytime help is, in effect, invisible help; that is, during evenings and weekends, the family can operate as a self-sufficient unit without ac-

6. Two other couples also had children, but they did not have childcare help. One couple's children lived with a former wife until they were in their early teens. The wife of another couple did freelance work from her home until her children were in school.

knowledging that it depends on and utilizes a third party. Perhaps, when both spouses work, day labor is a way to avoid confronting those contradictions that arise when the family is unable to operate as a self-sufficient nuclear family. Unable to make her help "invisible," one woman shifted from live-in help to day help:

> The first person we had was live-in. It was helpful in many respects, but I liked to come home and be alone. You've got to have enough room on two floors for this arrangement to work, and there just never seemed to be enough space. I wanted to get away and be with David, and the arrangement sort of dictated that we couldn't be on the first floor. I always felt I was being shoved off, so that she could clean or cook. I didn't like it at all. I was never raised with outside help, so we got rid of live-in help.

For these reasons, the majority of childcare workers do not live with the family that employs them. The most desirable workers, then, are those women who already have residences of their own. Teenagers and imported foreigners, the traditional live-in help of wealthy families, are less frequently employed by the couples in this sample. Older women or immigrant women already living in this country seem to comprise the two main childcare labor pools most amenable to daytime arrangements.

In an effort to accommodate the worker, children are not necessarily cared for in the couple's home (see Table 11). Whereas all foreign-born employees described in the interviews care for children in the couples' homes, only 58 percent of the native-born older women care for children there. The shift in childcare location was often a gradual one, as this woman described:

> My kids just liked the activity and stimulation at my sitter's home. I talked to a psychiatrist, because I'm really neurotic

TABLE 11. Location of Childcare for Day Workers

| *Category of Worker* | *Couple's Home* | *Worker's Home* |
|---|---|---|
| Teenagers and young girls (under age twenty-five) | 0% | 100% (3) |
| Older women | 58% (7) | 41% (5) |
| Immigrant women | 100% (5) | 0% |

NOTE: N = 20.

> about having somebody in my home with the kids versus them going to her home. I was advised that the important thing is that your sitter is comfortable in her environment. Clearly, they were all happier down there, and slowly they started spending all their time at the sitter's home. It got to the point that she'd come and get them in the mornings, and they would all walk back to her house.

In such cases the home environment of an older woman is considered a suitable place for children to spend the day, as many older women live in the same or an adjacent neighborhood. In the case of younger women, children may spend the day in either the childcare worker's home or in the couple's home. The closer the worker lives to the couple or the more similarity there is in social background, the more likely it is that her household will be used for childcare.

Being unaccustomed to hiring help, couples often lack knowledge about work parameters, such as whether the person they hire should care for their child exclusively or also do the housecleaning. This couple's inexperience resulted in their requesting only minimal services from their help:

> We made some mistakes when we hired her. We realize that now, but it was our first time. When she said, "What are my responsibilities other than taking care of the baby?" we said, "Just take care of the baby." Consequently, she does no household work, which is a pain because that means we do it on the weekends or I have to pay someone else to come in and do it. In our efforts to impress on this woman that we really wanted the baby taken care of, we went overboard in trying to compensate for the fact that we weren't going to be home with the baby ourselves.

The childcare worker's responsibilities vary from taking care of the child exclusively to combining childcare and household duties. Of course, those workers who care for the child in their own home are responsible only for childcare. These differences in responsibility are not related to amount of compensation. Workers who are only responsible for childcare are not necessarily paid less than workers who have additional responsibilities. Foreign help and teenagers are paid slightly less than older women. (Most couples, at the time of the interviews, paid $150 to $175 per week in cash, regardless of which category of worker they employed.) If the worker is responsible only for children, then couples may also employ an additional person to do the cleaning and laundry. Those who have daytime help will also often have teenage sitters one or two nights a week. And almost all parents, regardless of childcare arrangement, normally have their toddlers in a nursery school setting for part of the day.[7]

7. Floge (1985) examines changes in childcare arrangements experienced by mothers of preschool children over a four-year period. At the time of the initial interview, most childcare was provided by relatives, but over the course of this study, exclusive use of relatives declined sharply and was replaced by some form of group care (nursery school, daycare center, kindergarten) or a combination of arrangements that often included relatives. According to Floge, parents are more likely to use multiple-care arrangements as their children grow older.

Why do dual-career couples only hire daytime help rather than placing their children in the other types of daycare arrangements available? Hired childcare workers, even those who supposedly only work days, provide the couple with the flexibility their careers require. The childcare provider, who at times works twelve or more hours per day, is relied on to care for the couple's children until the parents return home. This male respondent, who pays over $10,000 a year for the care of his two children, described the service that his daytime sitter provides:

> What we are discovering is that when you have young kids and household help and you are paying that all in after-tax dollars, even if you are earning a lot of money your money is very scarce. And you want to get someone who's good and reliable. The gal we have is great. For example, she can be relied on to stay late when sometimes, unexpectedly, my wife or I don't get home till eight-thirty or nine o'clock. She stays till one of us gets there.

Therefore, hiring an individual childcare provider is an attractive alternative to other types of childcare options. And although it may appear to be an expensive option, these couples are purchasing flexibility, which cannot be provided by institutional services. A daycare center does not remain open if both parents have to work late, but an individual childcare worker can be expected to adapt to the special needs of each couple. Another man explained how the couple's changing career demands led to their decision to employ live-in help:

> [Employing live-in help] was triggered by our experiences. We actually had two babysitters before our second child was born, and they both came to our house and stayed there until we came home. We felt that with two children and with the prospect of greater travel than we had previ-

ously anticipated, that it would be better and more convenient for us to have somebody live in. It would give us more flexibility, and it wasn't any more expensive.

Although the general practice among couples is for one spouse to try to be home nightly with the children, this is not always possible. The flexibility of a hired childcare arrangement allows both spouses an equal opportunity to meet individual career demands, leaving them free, for example, to respond to extraordinary work circumstances and demonstrate their commitment to the corporate employer. Husbands and wives will often call each other in the late afternoon to confirm evening childcare arrangements in an effort to avoid having unforeseen work situations confound such arrangements. Childcare providers, whether they live in or work days, are expected to adapt at the last minute to their employers' special work needs, and in some cases if the sitter is unavailable, the sitter's family members may take charge of the child. One woman described the arrangement she and her husband have:

> We call each other in the afternoons, unless we have forewarning. I'll tell him I'm going to be late or he'll say, "I'm going to be late." And then we'll try to make arrangements. What we try to do is see that one of us gets home. But if that's impossible, we call the sitter; what's so nice about her is that she has a daughter about four years older than mine—fourteen—and if the mother's not around, her daughter can watch ours.

Once couples decide to hire an individual caretaker, the question becomes how to find such help, a problem that baffled these couples. One woman tackled it in the same way she solves problems in her corporate work. Finding a solution first demanded a little research. She called other working women in similar situations and found that numerous options existed for finding help.

> I didn't wait, unlike a lot of people who expect in two weeks all this will fall into place. Now, maybe it could, but it took me the better part of almost three months to come up with the ideal situation. I knew the daycares. I wanted to know the unique situations because they might really spring an idea. I called every working mother I knew, even if I didn't know them well, to find out what they were doing.
>
> I called the churches and I did go to the newspapers. I even found a couple this way who weren't bad. I did not call senior citizens' homes, although there are a lot of people doing that now, and they are getting people. . . . What I found that clicked was to call the really, really rich girls, because these girls inherit live-ins. And that is where I really got the connection. There is a group from Denmark; there is a group from Poland; there is a group from I forget where else. These pockets exist, and you can connect up with them. These girls are twenty-two years old, and they are responsible because they have to be cleared, etc., etc. It is a year of peace, and if you hook up properly, you keep getting them.

Instead of turning to professional organizations (which provide job training to certify these women) or to licensed organizations (which act as gatekeepers to filter out ill-suited childcare providers), these couples look for people without organizational affiliations. Co-workers or friends, bulletin boards or newspaper ads were the main sources for finding potential help.

> I put up a notice in the lobby of my building, hoping one of the women might know someone.

> My husband was out running and saw a sign on a bulletin board, saying childcare work wanted.

> I put an ad in the *Tribune* and found her.

> Through my boss's housekeeper, I found somebody.
>
> I always found somebody through a friend of a friend or from a housekeeper of a friend.

Couples turn to these other sources for finding help, in part because organizations do not yet have a monopoly over this type of labor, and therefore couples save a surcharge by locating workers independently. The term *organization* is used here to mean either an organization of childcare workers, such as a union, that exercises a monopoly over access to jobs and therefore negotiates on behalf of its members over issues such as wages, work rules, and working conditions; or, alternatively, a situation where the government certifies childcare workers, who then organize themselves as a professional group and, like doctors, lawyers, and accountants, use their certification to effectively negotiate from a much stronger position.

Instead of opting for organizations that assess the quality of the worker prior to employment, however, the couples I interviewed choose first to assess qualities of the individual and then to provide them with on-the-job instruction. This alternative more directly addresses the issue of control: when the socialization of domestic labor is provided after hiring, each worker can adapt to the unique needs of each family situation. The hiring of childcare providers, therefore, is based on "gut" or intuitive reactions to the personal qualities of an individual. As one woman recounted, "We advertised in the paper. We were just going by gut-level reaction. It is scary that you don't hear of more bad things happening, given how little insight you really have in terms of interviewing someone." Another explained simply, "We interviewed her and she was warm and loving." Both husbands and wives emphasized the personal qualities rather than the skills of the childcare providers when talking about their help.

It is ironic that reputation or occupational certification is the basis on which we select our lawyers, accountants, and doctors (with "bedside manner" as a bonus), and yet when childcare workers are selected, personal qualities become the main criteria. The childcare provider, unlike the physician, is not hired to provide specialized skills and knowledge. Rather, the childcare provider is hired as a substitute mother and is expected to act and react to the child in an individualized fashion, not according to an external organization's definition of proper childcare. These requirements reflect the couple's rejection of organizational or state intervention in the arena of childcare.

Removing early childhood care from the home is resisted by these couples. The earlier maternal responsibility of the biological mother for her young children now becomes either partially or fully delegated to another woman.[8] Therefore, hiring an individual surrogate rather than an organizational substitute allows parents to control the worker's socialization of their children. These workers are expected to act on behalf of their employers—the couple—not on behalf of an organization whose services the couple purchases. Furthermore, if we contrast the term *homemaker* with *housekeeper,* the former indicates the "maker" of the home and the latter the "keeper" of the home. In essence, dual-career couples, especially

8. Chodorow's *The Reproduction of Mothering* (1978) and Dinnerstein's *The Mermaid and the Minotaur* (1976) both focus on the psychological meanings and consequences of women's mothering and both argue that male *and* female parenting is essential for social change. The cases of the dual-career couples presented here have implications for this argument. In effect, the substitution of one woman for another will not significantly alter sex-role socialization. While children may learn that both mother and father go to work outside the home, women remain the primary childcare providers.

those who choose to hire live-in help, are attempting to turn those individuals who are keepers of the home into makers of the home.

### *Problems of Hired Labor: Turnover and Supervision*

Despite the attractiveness of the labor pools that provide childcare workers, the hired labor arrangement carries with it problems of worker instability and the need for supervision. Because these workers have few alternatives, the problems of keeping and controlling them would seem to be minimal. However, as many employers who require few skills and offer low pay have discovered, restricted opportunities for advancement and low economic rewards do not encourage employees to commit themselves either to the job or to the employer. Although there is considerable disagreement as to whether high turnover is the result of the type of job or a characteristic of disadvantaged workers, it is clear that "attractive" labor is not necessarily the most reliable or the easiest to control (Edwards, 1979).[9]

For dual-career couples, these problems are particularly acute. The availability of a stable and reliable childcare worker plays a major role in maintaining two careers, even when alternative childcare arrangements may be accessible. Insecurities associated with the loss of adequate childcare help can often be significant. As one respondent noted in describing the problem of turnover:

9. As described by the couples interviewed for this study, 30 percent of the childcare workers who left their employ quit to find alternative employment, 30 percent went back to their country of origin, and 15 percent were fired. Secondary reasons included homesickness on the part of a teenager, husbands graduating, and not wanting to care for older children.

While I've never developed an ulcer over work, I'm on my way to one over housekeepers. I think about housekeepers all the time. There has not been a day since Jean has been born that I don't have insecurities about losing help.

The costs associated with finding and then initiating a replacement worker can also be significant. Each time a worker leaves and another arrives, one or both members of the couple must take time off from work. In some cases they subtract the training period for childcare workers from vacation time, so as not to penalize their careers. To avoid being caught unprepared in a crisis situation, some people watch closely for signs of the imminent departure of help. Experienced couples claim they can tell when a worker is about to leave. One woman described this as a form of "street sense":

I've gotten very, very good at seeing the signs when someone's going to leave. They start shrugging responsibilities. I'm also able to gauge the [job] span of a particular person in terms of how long they will stay with us—being able to tell a lot of things right off the bat. It's like you develop a street sense about housekeepers. You just know how to tell with each individual what the story is going to be with them. Think about it. You develop things like a street sense when your survival depends on your developing these senses. My survival depends upon who is taking care of my child.

But even street sense cannot prevent the difficulties and adjustments presented by a labor force that is relatively unstable.

Parents' concern for the quality of their children's home environment also leads them to worry about the tendency toward low levels of commitment on the part of childcare workers. Many parents, stressing the importance of continuity in the relationship between their children and the childcare worker, unconsciously underscore the significance of the worker's duties. As one woman related:

> It would really make a lot of difference to me if I could keep somebody full-time, the same person. And then I think it's important to the children. Not only would it be disruptive to me if I were hiring a new person every couple of years, but look at it from the perspective of the children. I'm delegating a lot of authority and a lot of that responsibility. If it's a new person all the time, it's going to be tough on those children.

Whether or not continuity is indeed important for children, parents' belief in the psychological advantages of having the same worker around for an extended period of time makes the issue of turnover especially important. To the extent that childcare workers are seen as substitute authority figures, this problem becomes even more intense.

The problems of using a disadvantaged labor pool as the principal source of childcare workers are not limited to turnover but are also related to the high degree of responsibility attached to the job, coupled with the lack of direct supervision. The performance of a doctor or a lawyer can be evaluated on the basis of their past performances or can be inferred from their credentials and organizational membership; but few such methods are available for evaluating childcare workers. For example, only two couples in this study relied directly on a professional recruiting agency or investigated references prior to hiring a childcare worker. The lack of screening devices cuts both ways: on the one hand, the labor market is sufficiently disorganized to prevent the creation of professional groups; and on the other hand, the lack of such groups helps keep the price of childcare labor low. Nevertheless, parents have few means for monitoring the performance of the workers' duties, and they therefore rely heavily on the personal qualities and commitment of those workers. In earlier periods, the nanny or governess employed by the wealthy family had on-the-job supervision, as the wife was normally at home for at least part of the day. But for today's dual-career couples, what really goes on, especially with infants and young toddlers, is often completely unknown. Not many couples complained of bad experiences with unsupervised childcare workers, but few parents were completely free of concern for their child's well-being during their absence. Some parents expressed this concern by recounting the unfortunate experiences of friends or acquaintances with truly unreliable childcare workers. One woman cited an extreme example of a babysitter's negligence:

> I have a friend who had a baby, and one day she forgot something at home. So she went home, and her childcare person had her baby's head in the oven. And she said, "What are you doing to my baby?" and the childcare person said, "Well, I always do this. He seems to sleep better." And this is someone who lived in her house for six months, and who knows what the hell she did.

Stories such as this serve to remind parents of the paradoxical situation presented by hired childcare: great personal importance is attached to the position, but the childcare person is economically devalued. The activities and services these individuals provide are highly valued yet poorly rewarded—just as are the functions of homemakers in general.

The problems of turnover and supervision are, of course, classic ones for all employers. The solutions found by dual-career couples also reflect standard employer responses: (1) relying directly on external pressures, such as labor market competition or worker vulnerability, to exert control over worker performance; (2) offering higher wages to reduce turnover and to link the continuation of high wages to acceptable levels of performance; and (3) encouraging workers to develop a personal attachment to the job. Examples of each type of solution were discussed in the interviews.

In some cases couples use the disadvantaged status of their childcare workers as a means of exerting control. Recognizing that a worker's bargaining position is directly affected by her alternatives, some employers quash negotiations over such issues as wages and hours by confronting the worker with her vulnerability and lack of bargaining power. One couple, for example, took this approach with an undocumented immigrant who refused to work more hours:

> "We'd like to extend your hours," we told her, "and we'd like to give you ten extra dollars a week for the five extra hours." Well, math she knows, English she doesn't know. She goes through this whole thing—if she has to work more than nine hours, she wants time and a half. This was the craziest thing I'd ever heard in my entire life. She wanted time and a half—she wanted $175 a week. I told my husband to get rid of her. Well, these negotiations were like Sadat and Begin. It was crazy, but we went through them. Apparently she talked to some of her friends and she realized that, as she said, "I can go to work in a factory for $5 an hour." My husband said, "Fine. Go work for $5 an hour. By the time they take out taxes and you pay $40 a month for a bus pass, what do you think you are going to take home by the end of the week?" So apparently this must have gotten through, because she accepted our conditions.

Another couple used the undocumented status of their housekeeper to rationalize her low wages.

Legals would rather work in a factory. They can make more money than they can here, given what we are paying a housekeeper. Ours has got it in her head that after she has been here a year, she deserves a big raise. I'll probably give her another $10 a week. That will hopefully satisfy her. Anyway, she's illegal and can't get work elsewhere.

Other couples would pay above what they believe to be the prevailing wage in an effort to entice their workers to stay on. Perhaps in situations where couples are making highly variable or unpredictable demands, it is more important to have somebody—anybody. These couples are therefore willing to pay a higher wage in the hope that it will keep the worker from leaving. One woman explained why she pays her housekeeper a premium:

I pay $200 per week, which is above the market price. I consciously do that because I want to keep her. I mean, she's very good with the kids, a good combination of being very loving and very attentive but also very good on discipline. I have a lot of faith in her, and I want that continuity. And I carefully keep her wages above the going rate. I don't know what she could make in alternative employment. I think she likes working for us, but I consciously want to make sure that I pay her a premium to keep her, because I really hope that I can keep her all the way through the time I need childcare.

Others were quick to point out the perquisites they give their workers: "We pay her $185 plus birthday presents, Christmas presents, things that aren't normal." And still others told of the sorts of things they do so that their housekeeper will remain with them:

But we bend over backwards to keep her happy, not just in money terms. Holidays when she doesn't work—I certainly pay her for them. I give her two weeks' vacation. Whenever I get home early or my husband comes home early, we tell

> her to go. She feels funny. She doesn't want to, but we insist she goes. We do a lot of that, and I think you have to.

Although higher wages or more work-related benefits may be devices for engendering stability and rewarding proper performance, such practices are not described as the outcome of direct negotiation or the response to demands. Instead, they are "extended" by the employers in an effort to sustain the relationship. In this sense, the level of reward continues to be controlled by the employing couple.

Finally, the development of a personal attachment helps foster a nonmonetary and nonmarket basis for reducing turnover and increasing control. The use of personal attachment as a means of ensuring stability, however, is rarely recognized directly or consciously. As one woman described, some couples adopt a paternal role with respect to young women childcare workers:

> She came here strictly knowing that I'd take her twice a week to classes so that she could learn English. I sit with her at night and help her with her English. I feel very much like a surrogate mother to her. She's very good with our child, but emotionally she still needs somebody to be around; it's like having another teenager.

Another woman, however, related some of the disadvantages of assuming a parental role:

> If you find a fairly young person, you're going to end up in a parent role to them, and that quite often defeats the purpose for which you have them in your house; it certainly did in Cindy's case. We didn't throw her out, but the temptation was strong on many occasions. We just finally took her on as our project to see what we could do to help her stand on her own feet. We did become sort of substitute parents for her.

Others, such as the woman quoted below, described the development of a personal attachment between worker and child as the product of a voluntary effort by the worker:

> Right now I have an older woman who is a widow. For the last year she had been living with her daughter, who has teenage kids. The kids are always running from this practice to that. The daughter works and is one of these people who is terribly capable. The woman felt she didn't have anything to do. Nobody had any need for her. . . . I heard her saying to my daughter this morning, "Now Jenny, you should always put your napkin on your lap." I guess she is going to teach her how to be a lady. She loves her dearly and is always hugging and kissing her. She spends a lot of time reading and talking to her and taking her to the zoo and exposing her to a lot of culture.

In many cases, the integration of the worker as a quasi-member of the family seems a natural route to take, especially given the interaction fostered by the proximity of employer, employee, and child. One woman explained why she chose to treat her housekeeper as a member of the family:

> She's been here a year, and this is the longest I've ever had somebody. And in order to keep her, I had to make her feel very much like a member of the family. . . . She doesn't like to be responded to as a housekeeper. She likes to be responded to as a member of the family. For example, she gets really offended and upset if we say, "Do this," or "Get me that." But she will do it if asked nicely—but not when treated like a servant. . . . If they are sensitive enough to be a good person and take care of your child, then they're usually pretty sensitive about the way they're treated in the house.

In the following instance, this integration included the extended family as well:

> I know this couple that is so hung up about losing their help that they have allowed their twenty-three-year-old housekeeper to have her boyfriend move into their third floor. That's how afraid they were of losing her. They thought she was going to move in with him, so they fixed up the whole third floor for them and now he lives there with her. The boyfriend even goes on the train with the man in the morning. I find the whole arrangement bizarre.

This story is bizarre to the respondent because it goes beyond the boundaries of the hired labor relationship. However, childcare providers are often "incorporated" into the family as fictive kin and are referred to as surrogate aunts, mothers, and grandmothers. One man, explaining this surrogate relationship, said, "We have a super lady, who has sort of adopted the family and is down the block. The children get the same level of attention from their surrogate mother as they would from their mother or father." Some respondents described the extension of fictive kin status to the housekeeper's family as well.

> What ended up happening was—they live a few blocks from us. And first Sally would bring my daughter over to visit with her mother, and what ultimately happened was that she adopted my daughter as the grandchild she never had. Sally's brother and his wife adopted our daughter as the child they wished they had at that time. Then we got to be friends with all of them.

Claims based on family membership, then, make loyalty and trust, not wages, the basis of the relationship between couples and their childcare providers. One woman explained how she expects her housekeeper to act as a family member. Catching herself in her own word choice, she revealed that this relationship is not simply monetary:

> The one that I have right now, she is really a member of the family. I shouldn't call her "the one" or "the girl," because she's really a part of our family. I trust her implicitly. I trust her with my child, and there is nothing else in my life which is of more value. . . . She is really a part of our family, and I would really feel very hurt and very betrayed if she left.

In none of the instances cited above is the development of a personal bond—whether initiated by the employer or by the worker—viewed as something to be avoided. Rather, the worker's expression of attachment or interest is readily accepted because it serves as a further guarantee of the employee's stability. It also guarantees that the employee will make the parents'—and the children's—interests her own; and this is a major factor in improving quality as well as continuity of care. Just as employers in other settings may deny that their "concern" about employees' well-being represents paternalism as a form of control or that their efforts to integrate employees into the company (through company picnics or company-sponsored recreation) constitute manipulation, these couples do not see their actions as a form of domination. Indeed, many if not all seem quite sincere about what they view as their unselfish behavior. Nevertheless, paternalism, expressions of concern, and efforts to integrate workers into the family can increase the amount of control available to employers and therefore fulfill their goals of stability and reliability for the relationship. Of course, these strategies, whether used alone or in combination, are not entirely successful, as evidenced by continued problems of turnover.

### *Replacing the Wife*

The division of labor in the home is an important influence on individual career success. In the past particularly, male career success has been predicated on the existence of a nonworking wife (Whyte, 1956; Kanter, 1977). The "invisible work" of women, documented by many researchers (Smith, 1975–1976), was a major contributing factor to men's careers. Women's role was more than simply taking care of the hearth; the unpaid work wives did for their husbands' organizations also facilitated the husbands' career advancement. But most important, men were released from domestic responsibilities—both childcare and housework—so that they could concentrate their energies on meeting work-related goals. And wives provided two crucial services that complemented their husbands' work demands: they provided the stability of home life, and they were flexible and adapted to the special needs of the children's and husbands' respective worlds.

When both husbands and wives work, there is no one person whose primary responsibility is homemaking, a fact that the addition of children only emphasizes. From the corporate employer's point of view and, increasingly, from the couple's point of view, career success depends on a home life that does not preoccupy the worker. If *both* husbands and wives are to be released from domestic responsibilities, who will undertake these tasks? Perhaps more important, are the steps taken by these dual-career couples altering the traditional gender-based division of labor in the home?

In this section, I will argue that, at least among the couples interviewed, a shift in household responsibilities has indeed taken place. The traditional duties of the wife are changing; but the change represents not so much a transformation of responsibilities as a shift in who assumes them. Yet another shift involves the more general question of gender roles in the family. Wives have, to some extent, been released from the direct physical demands of childcare; but dual-career demands have not resulted in a shared process of recruitment and supervision of hired childcare or housecleaning labor. Rather, wives have assumed principal responsibility for these tasks.

Housekeepers and sitters are expected to provide the home with the stability that *should* relieve the couple from worry about family matters during workday hours. But because home duties remain, even for these couples, the domain of the wife, it is mainly wives who express such relief. This woman explains how her daytime sitter helps to stabilize her work concentration:

> The ideal is to have someone in your home—the ideal for the person working, because then you work harder. You are not worried about what is going on at home. People are not calling you to tell you about your kids, which happens frequently at daycare. I know because I work with people in that situation. You don't have to run and pick them up if they are throwing up, or whatever. All that kind of stuff relieves you to do a good job, and that is what I think you pay for.

Women did point out that their housekeepers or daytime sitters were replacements for themselves during work hours. The paid surrogate assumes the wife's responsibilities, as one woman described:

> She comes to my home every day at seven-thirty in the morning, and she leaves when I get home at six or six-thirty. She does everything for me. She does the cleaning and household chores. She does the things that I would do if I were there. She feeds my daughter. She really takes

> care of her. For example, she cuts her hair, and she is there when my daughter's friends come over to play.

Cloistering wives in the home is unthinkable for dual-career couples. Instead, both husbands and wives spend their days working outside the home, and the housekeeper/sitter is a paid replacement for the wife. She is now the person who keeps daily watch over the home. Even when parents feel their children are old enough for nursery school, full-time, day, or live-in housekeepers still offer an advantage, especially when women have erratic work hours or when their work cycle includes a busy season. Housekeepers can adapt to these needs, and more important, there is always someone at home. One woman illustrated this point:

> I'm starting my son in nursery school in the mornings, and in the afternoon he's in a play group. I'd like to keep him one-on-one with someone in the house as long as I can. I'm not so afraid now of what would happen if my housekeeper quit, because he's under the supervision of other options during the day. I like the fact that she's at home all day long, though. But I need her at night. There are nights when I wouldn't be home till twelve o'clock, and there are nights when it might be better not to come home at all—during my busy season, it's easier for me to stay downtown.

Home repairs, such as fixing broken appliances or clogged plumbing, have also traditionally been taken care of by wives who were home during the hours repairmen work. But the handling of such repairs is now the domain of this surrogate, especially of those women who work in the couple's home, relieving wives of the burden of contending with these chores. One woman explained why the ability to handle these problems was a prerequisite in a housekeeper: "I also wanted someone who could care for the house—not only clean—but something like if the lock breaks, she could call a locksmith. Why should I have to worry about it?"

Similar to the homemaker wife, domestic helpers can determine how they use their time. As long as responsibilities are met and childcare remains their priority, the specifics of their time management are not questioned. When I asked what the sitter did all day long, one respondent said:

> She is just here [at home]. She comes in the morning and sends my daughter off to school. Then she does what she wants. I have never been dissatisfied with how she cleans or does the laundry, so I don't ask what she does.

Housekeepers are expected to provide home stability, not only by performing household tasks but also just by their presence in the home. Yet this stability is cause for constant concern among the career women who employ hired help.

Housekeepers and sitters are not simply performing the traditional role of wife and mother. If this were the case, both spouses would be equally freed by hired labor to pursue careers, and both would be equally responsive to and responsible for their workers. In this regard, a gender-based division of labor, at least for dual-career spouses, would not exist. Instead, what appears to be a symmetrical relationship between a childless husband and wife may be deceptive; and a division of labor allegedly not based on gender is definitely challenged when the couple decides to have children. For example, when these couples had no children and the cleaning person failed to show up, the house could remain uncleaned. But such neglect is not possible when the sitter fails to show up; children need continuous care. Incorporating children into the family's structure entails a reorganization of the couple's joint and separate lives that results in the resurrection of an asymmetrical relationship—that is, housekeepers and sitters become primarily the wife's responsibility. Normally, it is the wife who finds the help, indoctrinates the help, worries about losing the help, and daily converses with the help. As one woman angrily complained:

> My husband has never lost a day's work or a night's sleep over insecurities about help. It has never entered my husband's head that this would have any effect on his career. He has never interviewed a housekeeper. He's never had this affect his life in any way, shape, or form.

Wives are the ones who rearrange work schedules and normally report having more flexible careers. They are either more willing to figure out flexible work arrangements, or they are more apt to change jobs to regularize their work hours. They are, as one woman explained, charged with relieving the housekeeper from her duties:

> Since my schedule is the much more predictable one, it's my schedule that I coordinate. So I stay. Generally, I stay in the morning till she comes, and then when I come in the evening—I'm usually the first person home—she leaves then.

Wives, therefore, are the ones who really provide their husbands with continuous flexibility. And, in turn, the housekeeper provides the wife with flexibility.

The problems of turnover and the unstable nature of housekeepers are regarded as wives' problems. Wives thus express more insecurity about losing this help because such a loss would immediately and directly disrupt their work lives. For example, each new childcare worker must be initiated into her responsibilities, and it is the wife who must take time off from work, staying home during this period of sitter adjustment. In an effort to avoid penalizing their careers, wives may take vacation time for this training period. One woman explained why she has not taken a "real" vacation since her child was born three years ago:

> Every time I get a new housekeeper, I will spend a period of time at home to stay with her while she gets to know my son, while she gets to know my house and everything else. So, for every new housekeeper, I have to count a vacation week out of work, which results in my never taking vacation time because it doesn't accumulate.

Furthermore, when the housekeeper or sitter fails to meet her daily responsibilities, the husband's work life is rarely disrupted. If the sitter arrives late in the morning, the wife is the one who will have to answer to clients and bosses and rearrange her work schedule. One woman has live-in help mainly to avoid this potential problem in the winter.

> I wanted live-in help because I didn't want the fear of—for example—on a snowy winter day at eight-thirty in the morning not having my help come in to take care of the baby when I have to be in the office. We very rarely go out at night during the week. First of all I'm tired, and I haven't seen my daughter all day, and I like to be with her. So there isn't a need to have live-in help to babysit. I could get around having live-in help if it weren't for the fact that I need to know someone is there in the mornings.

Couples prenegotiate these structural arrangements, and although wives are the ones expected to take time off from work when housekeepers or children are sick, husbands may help out for short periods in an emergency or when other back-up systems are unavailable. One man described the arrangement he and his wife had negotiated.

> We have worked it out that when it comes to the kids, she's on the line first. If it is really touch-and-go, like the kids are sick, Sally will stay home. If she were out of town or something, which occasionally she will be, and they were sick, I would just stay home if it was required. Anyone in this firm can take a day off for personal reasons without being docked or having it charged to vacation time. But it hasn't happened, because we have two healthy kids.

Another man's responsibility when childcare arrangements fail is to "help my wife think of somebody she can call."

Sometimes, husbands and wives will jointly interview a potential sitter or housekeeper. But it is the wives who have already done the "leg work," made the connections, and weeded out unsuitable individuals. In terms of who makes decisions about hiring childcare providers, one husband said, "I would say that it's more her decision—80 percent her decision and 20 percent my decision. I would just have a little input. She would make the ultimate decision."

These comments further underscore the fact that hiring childcare labor is a female responsibility. Women are no longer doing the actual housework or caring for the child all day long; instead, they are now one step removed, overseeing the work their mothers did in the past. "Replacing the wife," therefore, is not simply a metaphor for describing the role of hired labor, but it also indicates the tenuous position of the dual-career female—at any time the wife can be recalled to the home to reassume homemaking activities.

Working women need to trust and feel secure about their hired labor in order to feel that they exert some control over the childcare situation. Without this trust, they cannot effectively replace themselves with a housekeeper; and if they cannot, then the whole point of having an independent career is undermined. But despite the critical elements of trust, these wives do rely on what is generally an unpredictable and unregulated labor market. They build trust based on systems of hiring and payment that have few if any guarantees of performance. For this reason, housekeepers and sitters are often given quasi-family membership and a relationship of reciprocal loyalty and trust is developed. To encourage the childcare worker to assume part of the mother's traditional responsibility and to maximize the stability and continuity of the parent-worker-child relationship, the relationship between employer and employee must be something more than the exchange of a wage for a service.

Although extended kin play an important but secondary role in the organization of these dual-career families, they do not relieve the wife of the general responsibility for recruiting and supervising hired labor. Family does provide a back-up system for hired labor when a crisis develops. For example, if the couple's sitter suddenly quits, grandparents can become pinch-hitters, as one woman described: "Each time a sitter left, I would face the tragedy and call my mother; she'd come here and stay till I found someone else." Even though relatives do not always live nearby, the knowledge that the potential for help exists can ease fears.

> A couple of times both the housekeeper and the kids were sick, and we've had a back-up, a back-up from a sitter service. If we were really pushed, we could use family, but they are forty-five minutes away. So it would mean that if we couldn't get anyone, that is what we would do theoretically. I would leave at six o'clock and drive the kids up there and be back to start work by eight. It's possible, although we've never done it. But it is part of the reason we feel more secure.

One woman did calculate, however, that in an emergency it would be cheaper to fly her in-laws to Chicago than to pay for a babysitting service.

> My real emergency back-up support system is my husband's folks. I know if there was ever a real emergency, like if the sitter quit all of a sudden and I didn't have a replacement, they would be out the next day if I paid their airfare. This would be cheaper than the prices I checked out for a babysitting service. His parents are my real fail-safe device. They are both retired and they aren't locked into anything.

Grandparents also provide a place for young parents to go if they need to get away from the chaos of managing children and careers. As one woman said, "If it just gets too much to handle and one of us ourselves needs a parent, that's where we go."

Extended kin may also help out during the worker's vacation. During two separate interviews, couples received calls confirming such plans. As one woman told me after the interview was interrupted for the call, "We are fortunate that my husband comes from a large family and that there are women in his family that are available to help out." Several couples' parents had moved to the Chicago area to be close to children and grandchildren. They would mainly take children for the weekend and would sometimes babysit during evenings. One woman explained why she tries to have family members stop by when she and her husband are out of town at the same time:

> So we make arrangements with my parents or my sister and her husband, who only live one mile away. We try to make arrangements with somebody in the family to come over and visit so there is something special for the kids in it.

Those couples without geographically close family members rely on babysitting services or neighbors for emergency situations. Nonworking mothers in the neighborhood may also watch children if the need arises.

## CONCLUSION

On the surface, dual-career couples *appear* to be able to operate as a self-sufficient nuclear family. Nonetheless, they are dependent as a group and as individuals on a category of people external to the family. Couples view their ability to purchase this service as another indication of their self-sufficiency (or "making it"). Yet appearances are deceptive, because the self-sufficiency of the dual-career couple depends on a system external to the family. What appears to be self-sufficiency for one category of workers relies on the existence of a category of less advantaged workers. What appears to be progress for women is really the progress of some women at the expense of equal progress for other women.

Fusfeld (1973) argues that the low-wage economy of urban ghettos plays a significant role in the overall economy of the larger metropolitan area. In analyzing the position of middle-income groups, he states:

> If wages are raised in the low-wage industries, the cost of living will rise and their standard of living will fall. Many people are aware of this relationship, although it is usually expressed in some phrase such as, "someone has to wash the dishes," or "who will collect the trash?" (32–33).

The relationship between housekeepers and these dual-career couples is analogous. Two incomes are necessary for these couples to maintain their lifestyle, but even with the cost of hiring domestic labor, the lifestyle of the dual-career couple is more affluent than that of their one-income family counterparts. Hiring domestic labor is not an equal exchange of one spouse's salary in return for work in the home. Dual-career couples have an indirect but material interest in maintaining an unstable, low-wage pool of labor, in part because the couples place a high value on affordable, private childcare. For women to replace themselves with domestic help, their income must be large enough to make their work outside the home financially worthwhile. If the wages of domestic help were raised to accord with the value placed on childcare, the question of why this work was being farmed out would arise, even if higher wages produced a more stable and more skilled labor supply. Paying more would not only result in a decline in the standard of living for these couples but would also call into question the value of women's working outside the home.[10] Thus, the relation between domestic labor and dual-career couples represents one aspect of the more generalized and structured relationship of inequality between low-wage labor in the urban ghettos and high-wage labor in the middle- and upper-class neighborhoods and suburbs. This relationship, though often obscured by a focus on individual or group characteristics, is nonetheless important in understanding how such phenomena as dual-career couples with children are possible within modern society.

10. After taxes a woman must earn about twice what she pays her help in order to break even. When couples have a joint accounting system, the costs for childcare are usually subtracted from the wife's salary instead of being evenly divided between the two spouses. Even though the money may be pooled, the wife's contribution is not considered as her gross income but rather as her gross income minus childcare and housecleaning costs, which reduces the value of her work, and therefore her worth, considerably. In these instances, women are expected to foot the bills for childcare even if they do not provide the care themselves. When couples have separate accounting systems, childcare costs are divided between the two spouses as part of the common pot. However, I suspect that if childcare costs rose significantly, even these couples would be forced to reevaluate the advantages of the wife remaining in the labor force.

# 6
# THE DUAL-CAREER COUPLE: Implications and Future Directions

IN CONTRAST to the myth and hyperbole surrounding the "modern couple," this study has attempted to analyze the opportunities and constraints faced by the dual-career marriage and family, stressing the relationship between work, family, and gender as a way to emphasize the reciprocity between *autonomy* and *contingency* for individuals, couples, and social classes. The marriage of two careers and incomes has bought a measure of autonomy for these couples and for the individuals involved. As a couple, they can pursue a lifestyle unprecedented for anyone but the rich; as individuals, they are less subject to the vagaries of a single source of income, less dependent on the success of one career. Yet the existence of the dual-career marriage and family is contingent on the availability of career positions, outside labor to perform household and childcare chores, and, perhaps most important, the capacity of couples to adapt themselves to competing employer demands. These couples experience the interplay between autonomy and contingency as a series of difficult choices.

This study also offers an important insight about how ideologies are shaped by changes in social structures and institutions. The dual-career couples in this study have not consciously chosen a new relationship or family form because of some revolutionary shift in their beliefs or attitudes toward the family or male-female relationships. Rather, their pursuit of career success, financial well-being, and self-sufficiency is an attempt to play out their (and their parents') version of the American dream. Having graduated from college into the era of women's liberation, the women in this study are more aware of the available possibilities. Likewise, the men were not unaffected by the women's movement. But such possibilities had to materialize in the form of careers for women—careers that were an intersection of feminism and the American dream. It was the possibility of achievement and independence rather than the desire to make a political statement that pushed these women to have careers.

Once married, two-career couples must come to grips with both the externally imposed demands of the organizations that employ them and the lack of an appropriate ideology to guide them in creating marital relationships. The ideology of the traditional family simply does not work—the wife cannot stay home and do the housework. But it is not political (feminist) ideology that leads these couples to construct new marriages or new approaches to marital roles; instead, their employers' demands and their own desires for individual and combined career success lead them toward these changes. The ideology of equality, particularly in marital roles, emerges out of common opportunities and constraints, not out of a prior commitment to a feminist philosophy.

This point is crucial. It is a common misunderstanding that all one needs to do is wish or want another way of life and that somehow marriages, family, work, or even politics will be altered by our dreams and desires. This study demonstrates that these lifestyle "pioneers" did nothing of the sort; they reconstructed family forms not because they desired to blaze new social trails but because the constraints of work and the value placed on success altered the practices of their daily lives. Once established, these practices give rise to new ideologies of marriage and the family.

This chapter begins with a clarification of the class and family context in which the dual-career couple must be understood, draws together major findings about dual-career couples, offers suggestions for future research, and concludes by focusing on the implications that merging two careers has for the future of the marital bond.

## CLASS AND FAMILY STRUCTURE

To most outside observers, the couples in this study would probably appear "successful." They all have careers and seem destined to occupy increasingly privileged positions. As individuals and as families, they rank near the top of the income pyramid. Each couple has, to this point at least, navigated the choppy waters of a two-career marriage and maintained a viable relationship. Some have even managed to integrate careers, marriage, and children.

Yet, the term *successful* is misleading because it implies the existence of an ideal situation or ideal type against which marriages can and should be measured. If high incomes, high-status jobs, and durable marriages are the ideal, then these couples would probably be judged as successful. However, if other criteria—such as a strong commitment to home life and traditional marital relations—are valued, then it is not clear that the dual-career couples of this study would be judged so favorably. Success is a subjective valuation, and this subjectivity affects both the criteria used and the applicability of the term to different situations. If, as many sociologists have argued, objective factors (such as one's income, gender, race, or family background) affect the evaluative frame one adopts (what one values or devalues), then it is conceivable that for some readers these couples are far from successful. These cautionary statements are intended to suggest that for people in categorically different situations (for example, different social classes), what is considered successful might often be tempered by what is possible. These couples are successful in integrating careers and marriage and in questioning traditional gender roles largely because it has been possible for them to do so; such opportunities may be unattainable for others.

These distinctions are more than just semantic points. Work, family, and gender roles, far from being independent of one another, are interactive and mutually determining. Because these dual-career couples occupy social and organizational positions that carry with them high earnings and continued upward mobility, they are set apart from other categories of families. These social and monetary advantages allow, although they do not require, differences in family organization and gender roles, in comparison to other families. Money may make a difference in the way families are organized and in the social relations between husbands and wives, but the structure of work and occupations and the economy in general are responsible for the differential distribution of money and wealth.

Compare, for instance, the experiences of these upper-middle-class dual-career couples with those of the work-

working-class couples interviewed by Rubin (1976).[1] The "worlds of pain" that working-class couples experience contrast dramatically with the world experienced by dual-career couples. Desiring release from conflict and tension in their parents' home, young working-class men and women attempt to gain independence by rebelling, having early sexual experiences, and establishing their own individual lifestyles. Yet, as Rubin shows, the flight from parental restriction and economic dependence often leads to other and more oppressive bonds: a lack of sexual experience (particularly for women) and early pregnancy channel many young couples into marriage and parenthood. Early family responsibilities, combined with inadequate formal education, yoke working-class husbands into lower-status, dead-end jobs; working-class wives are saddled with children, and, because of their lack of skills, have extremely limited opportunities for continued education or subsequent investment in work-related skills. Men can struggle to improve their family's

1. Rubin's study, intended to document and explain the struggles of working-class families, was built on an explicit comparison with the life experiences and values of middle-class managerial and professional families, arguing that a family's class position largely determined its economic resources and opportunities and, by extension, the relations between husbands and wives. However, two factors impeded the class-based comparison. First, data on the two classes of families were uneven. Although neither group was randomly selected, far more detail was presented on working-class families, whereas middle-class families tended to be depicted in broader terms. Thus, a systematic comparison could not be constructed, and class-based explanations of differences were less convincing than they might have been. Second, a conceptual framework for understanding social stratification by class was lacking. Conceptualizing the connection between class and family structure is by no means an easy undertaking, largely because the connection is indirect (as suggested in Chapter 1). Rarely are the relations among classes of families direct—even when one employs or purchases the labor of another—in the same sense that there is no immediate, tangible connection between rich and poor neighborhoods. Thus, in Rubin's analysis, the "worlds of pain" in which working-class couples live are not produced by middle-class couples; yet these couples are connected by their relation to an underlying economic system that creates them both.

economic lot; but cyclical unemployment, tiring work, and organizational barriers to white-collar work create an iron curtain that prevents escape from the working class.

The result, as Rubin argues and the couples themselves describe, is a situation in which the family becomes a social and psychological pressure cooker. Husbands, seemingly blocked at every turn in their struggle to fulfill the American dream, become angry and frustrated and blame themselves; in some cases, they turn to alcohol and abuse their wives and children. Wives, living with financial insecurity and their husbands' anger and frustration, respond with anger and frustration of their own, often venting their feelings on husbands and children. Children simply experience a repeat of their parents' early years and adolescence.

Although some came from working-class families, the dual-career couples in this study were able to avoid early entrapment in marriage, children, and jobs. The time they spent at college provided sufficient opportunity to experiment (both sexually and intellectually) without the threat that such experiments would turn into inescapable obligations. Their diplomas, social networks, and college work experiences opened doors to a broader set of possibilities than existed for their working-class counterparts. Their work demanded commitment and responsibility, but then rewarded these efforts with higher income, security, and opportunities for real advancement. The American dream, as many expressed it in Chapter 3, came quickly and in some instances unexpectedly.

It might be argued that dual-career couples have something working-class couples lack: motivation, ambition, or desire. But it would be a mistake to overlook the ways in which such "traits" are acquired: from parents whose resources made college possible; from instructors and peers who encouraged these individuals in college; from employers who offer enticements and incentives; and from their pleasurable lifestyle itself, which requires continued effort to sustain it. The women in this study offer the best evidence against using inherent motivation as an explanation for why some people get ahead and others do not. In describing their career beginnings (Chapter 2), many women claimed that they had no plans for careers while in college or, in some instances, after college. Careers "emerged" in various ways, primarily through labor market shifts but also through husbands' encouragement and, significantly, through the recognition by these women that they could do the work they saw others (men) doing.

These points are not intended to devalue motivation or the accomplishments of dual-career couples. Rather, they are intended to focus attention on the systematic difference in objective circumstances and possibilities that face people from different social classes. The advantages dual-career couples enjoy and build on do not result from their direct exploitation of working-class couples or the working-class wives who perform household and childcare chores. Instead, the class structure that results from the organization of the economy into owners and managers on the one hand and workers on the other creates two distinct groups in relation to household and childcare services: those who need the work done but do not have the time to do it, and those who have little alternative but to do it for pay. Hiring labor is only one possibility that enables dual-career couples to save time. Yet, hiring the labor of working-class women tangibly creates a relationship that already exists at an underlying social structural level.

If family structure is understood within the context of class-stratified society, then a similar argument must be made concerning gender. Without recapitulating the extensive debates among feminists and leftist theoreticians on the relationship between gender and class inequalities, it is undeniable that the opportunity for women in this study to pursue careers is partially dependent on the availability of other women to work in the home.[2] As women often pointedly argued in chapters 4 and 5, day-care workers are essential to maintaining the household; moreover, they make it possible for career women to organizationally and economically compete with men and at the same time strive for the personally and socially valued status of mother. Career women are making a rational set of choices in the face of organizational demands; they do not consider hiring labor to be exploitative. The issue is not that some women hire other women and thereby exploit them. (Indeed, the increasing numbers of career women and dual-career households have created a small boom in the employment market for unskilled labor.) Rather, the ability of dual-career couples to enjoy the privileges of careers is predicated on the availability of lower-paid household and childcare workers; that is, on a systematic and unequal distribution of advantages and disadvantages.

It is not inconceivable that other categories of families could achieve a measure of the equity between husbands and wives that I found among these dual-career couples. However, the structure of work and the opportunities available to those other families reduce the possibility that society-wide equality would result. For example, in a family situation where only the husband works outside the home, earns a modest income, and has little likelihood of significant increases in his earning power over

2. For such debates, see Hartmann, 1981a, 1981b; Mitchell, 1966; Firestone, 1970; and the recent collection of critical essays edited by Keohane et al., 1982.

time, the wife may be trapped in a situation in which her labor in the home is necessary simply to sustain the family as a viable unit. Such a division of labor would be experienced not as a conscious choice but instead as the product of an economic system that values the man's activity less than that of many others (such as managers) but more than the wife's. The subjective valuation of that division of labor reinforces the inequality between husband and wife and replicates the general system of economic inequality that has created a hierarchy of families.

## THE MARRIAGE OF CAREERS

The focused examination of a particular type of family—the dual-career family—has made it possible to consider the relationship of work, family, and gender roles against the backdrop of the broader system of class and economic inequality. Particular attention has been devoted to family organization and gender roles in situations where class is held constant; that is, whether more equal relations between husbands and wives, and between men and women in general, develop when partners in a marriage have relatively equal status and income. What follows here is a summary of the findings and implications of this study as they pertain to family and gender roles.

### *Family*

Middle-class notions of family self-sufficiency and autonomy are myths. Even with their financial resources, dual-career couples must purchase individual and institutional services in order to fulfill traditional family functions. The image of self-sufficiency masks the wide range of private exchanges between dual-career couples and other actors in the socioeconomic system on whom these couples depend. Because arrangements for these services are made privately, the myth of self-sufficiency is maintained. Conversely, the desire for such self-sufficiency directs the effort to fulfill these functions into the private sphere. The solutions these couples have implemented run counter to the feminist and Marxist visions of the consequences of women's entry into the labor force, namely, that women's participation would lead to demands for the communal satisfaction of domestic needs. Instead of demanding that private domestic needs be made public, these women have insisted on keeping domestic services private—partly because there are few collective services available and partly to perpetuate the image of self-sufficiency promised by sizeable income. In effect, they have brought the market into the home instead of taking the housework into the market.

Money does not buy self-sufficiency. On the contrary, money ties these people into the economic system in a different way than it does for those who have fewer resources. Dual-career couples trade time for money, and, instead of bartering their own labor with friends and relatives as lower-class families do (Stack, 1975), they buy domestic services from strangers. Moreover, they are trapped into a system in which they require two incomes to make the purchases they desire. This system may be seen as a "treadmill of reproduction," analogous to Schnaiberg's (1980) "treadmill of production." Their lifestyle has been inflated to the point where both incomes are necessary to maintain their way of life and to ensure the persistence of their high-level jobs.

Couples fully recognize the necessity of two incomes

when they contemplate having children. The decisions to have children, when to have them, and how to care for them are the most difficult family issues these couples face. Rarely do other personal or family problems infringe on work demands to the extent that child-related issues do. Yet, corporate (and professional) career trajectories are still based on the assumption that there is one type of family—the traditional nuclear family. Even though the gender composition of the corporate work force has changed, the demands and structure of careers within these firms have remained relatively static. Thus, career women postpone childbearing until they have been promoted to higher ranks in their firms. There is little evidence that women who want to have children make it in the corporate world; those who have children prior to critical career promotions are often later denied these promotions. The heavy career investment these women must make early in their work lives leads to the postponement of children, and thus they do not combine working with childbearing in the early stages of their careers. Therefore, employers share responsibility for, yet are unresponsive to, the timing of the birth of children to the women they employ. Further, the corporate environment prevents women from voicing collective concerns and demands by making individual deals and special arrangements with the few women who are seen as indispensable to the organization.

Pushed into a corner by their career demands and desire to succeed, these couples (and women in particular) face anxieties for which few social scientists have ready responses. Two concerns are paramount for these couples. First, the timing of children causes couples to worry about how to synchronize biological and career clocks. There are no convenient pauses in either timeframe, and as couples seek to establish their careers, time threatens to run out.[3] The second concern is for the potential long-term consequences for children of the dual-career family environment. In chapters 4 and 5 couples hinted at their fear that their children will lack nurturance—social or psychological—when both parents are away from home all day, and sometimes into the night. These fears have caused many couples to use what is popularly called "quality time" with their children as a way to salve their consciences and as a response to a society that tends to be unfavorably predisposed against surrogate childcare. Without definitive clinical or scientific evidence about the effects of parental absence from the home, anxieties grow, and couples seek individual solutions rather than making demands on employers for more time with their families.

When these couples bring other individuals into the nuclear family for childcare and housekeeping, there are important though unintended consequences. Fictive kin ties are created, even if the relationships are expected to exist only for short periods of time. For example, many couples found themselves involved in the personal and family lives of people they hired and sometimes helped solve problems for these people—lending money, finding housing, helping with bureaucratic intricacies, and socializing with employees' relatives—largely out of a vested interest in keeping their hired help. Regardless of motive, however, this effort involved these couples in new and unanticipated networks.

3. A related issue involves the potential burden faced by children whose parents are approaching retirement. Couples who have their first child in their mid- to late thirties could eventually prove a financial or emotional burden later in life, just as their children are embarking on their own careers. This issue clearly deserves further research.

A final point concerning family focuses on the issue of stability. Middle-class and upper-middle-class one-career families employed by corporations in past decades have achieved economic stability at the expense of geographic stability. This is not the case for these dual-career couples, who have remained geographically rooted in the Chicago area. Chicago is a major corporate city in which two careers can thrive without repeated geographic disruption. But more important than Chicago's career opportunities is the dual-earner character of these marriages. Spouses are not forced to relocate at the whim of their employing firm; instead, they have more freedom to switch careers and to be more selective about career moves because the other spouse's career acts as a backstop. The conjoining of two careers in one marriage enhances the likelihood of geographic stability for this group.

### *Gender Roles*

Interviews conducted for this study strongly suggest that concerns about equity between husbands and wives rarely precede the construction of the dual-career marriage. The practice of combining two careers rather than the adherence to a nonsexist ideology informs change. In this respect work is the leading factor shaping the domestic sector. Two careers shape the career marriage, but at some point the career marriage may begin to impinge on the two individual careers and in turn shape them. In the process, gender roles can be altered.

Although work creates external pressure for equality between spouses, there is no guarantee that equity within the home will result from career equity. I have highlighted two aspects of this problem: the type of budgets that couples implement, and the differing values attached to fathering versus mothering roles. A large income does make a difference in husband-wife relations. How that money is conceptualized and used by the couple, however, continues to play a crucial role in power relations between husbands and wives. Equity and equal salaries alone cannot change relations between spouses.

The division of labor in the home is transformed simply because equal work demands are made on husbands and wives. However, until the status of housework is elevated or, more important, until fathering acquires an equivalent normative meaning for men, women will continue to be responsible for childrearing (and to feel the corresponding guilt over working, something husbands do not share). Rarely did fathers in these couples talk about fathering as important to them; however, the women placed great importance on mothering as something they *should* provide. Therefore, an asymmetry still exists between husbands and wives in terms of parenting, further reinforced by a cultural ideology and social norms that applaud women for having careers, yet react with horror when mothers continue to work while their children are young (Fraiberg, 1977).

Because the existence of more high-powered careers for women is relatively recent, women are more likely to be glad they have a career than to push for compensation equal to their male co-workers'. Some women even believe that they must work harder to prove their commitment to their employers, and how they handle maternity leaves can become a "test of manhood." For the immediate future, these women look for equity in a more immediate environment—at home, with their husbands. The problems of equity between men and women in general are more distant and much more amorphous. Thus, the problems of sexual politics are still being staged behind closed doors. It is ironic that in order for gender differences to *significantly* decline, there must be relative equity in incomes and in work between husbands and wives.

### *Corporate Employers: The Silent Partners*

This study has emphasized how the partners in dual-career couples negotiate, bargain, trade, and occasionally battle with each other in an effort to shape work, marriage, and children into a complex but livable arrangement. Couples are required to make these adjustments because, with few exceptions, employers have not felt compelled to respond to the new phenomenon of dual-career marriage. At this point most positive responses by employers have been exceptions to the rule (such as special dispensations for pregnant female executives). Negative corporate responses, which are often continuations of out-of-date restrictive policies, are such that they "prevent" the corporation from having to respond to changed circumstances (such as the decision to have no maternity leave policy). Corporations define these matters as non-issues or nonproblematic (Spector and Kitsuse, 1977). Even less direct challenges to corporate policy—such as refusals to relocate as part of a dual-career strategy—have not been dealt with systematically by most employers. In the experiences of the respondents in this study, such refusals are commonly treated either as momentary indiscretions (which can be overlooked by a compassionate boss) or as signals that the employee in question is not as "serious" as his or her co-workers. And, as many people in this study stated, they will go to great lengths to keep their jobs, even if there is a price for having children or a spouse with a career. In short, corporations treat these matters as private troubles rather than as social issues (Mills, 1959).

Corporate employers have been and still remain the silent (and relatively intransigent) partners in the dual-career marriage. But the deals they strike with their employees are not intended to promote dual-career marriage, only to condone it if it is necessary to satisfy a given valued employee. Thus, it is left to the couple to accommodate the contradictions, pressures, and dissatisfactions of the corporate world and to build a wall around themselves in order to survive the double demands made on them by their employers. The result, ironically, is these couples' increased emphasis on the marriage as a third career. But this career must buffer the couple from outside pressures *and* act as a selective membrane that allows only part of the world to permeate into the home environment.

## THE FUTURE OF DUAL-CAREER MARRIAGE

In view of the complex struggles in which these couples engage—with each other as well as with employers, children, relatives, and employees—it is remarkable that dual-career marriages even exist. But do they have a future? This study in itself cannot adequately answer this question; only intact couples were interviewed, and only past and current experiences could be analyzed. However, several findings can be put together to generate some hypotheses for future research.

In contrast to the normative model of the traditional marriage, the majority of couples in this study did not base a family division of labor on separate spheres of activity and experience. The traditional role of breadwinner and, by extension, husband is shared by both men and women. Neither can claim that status solely, by virtue of equivalent career demands, and neither can be relegated to the position of nonproductive spouse. Thus, the traditional implicit exchange between husbands and wives—he supports the family economically and in exchange she maintains the home—is abrogated. The couples in this study demonstrate that an independent income brings to the surface questions of equity and symmetry that are largely unheard of and often actively discouraged in the traditional family. The keeping of separate financial accounts makes the equity issue more visible. Husbands can no longer legitimate their authority over financial and political matters on the basis of their greater experience with or knowledge of the outside world. In dual-career marriages, both partners have intimate knowledge of that world.

Following the logic of the traditional model, the dual-career marriage has no future. Aside from the stresses of two careers, the disruption of the traditional exchange between husbands and wives and the radical break with a "complementarity of roles" (Parsons and Bales, 1955) should be enough to subject the marriage to unbearable pressures. When the function of the wife as provider of childcare and early childhood socialization is diminished as substantially as it is in the families interviewed here, then the fate of the dual-career marriage would seem bleak.[4]

4. A number of readers and audiences to whom this research has been presented reacted quite negatively to the strategies some of these dual-career couples adopt in dealing with money, household affairs, and children. Many of these people, including some partners in academic dual-career marriages, objected that separate accounting systems reflect "crass materialism" and a step toward marital dissolution. The vehemence of their reactions reveals first, I would suggest, their understandable ignorance of the circumstances of corporate employment. As the dual-career couples convincingly argue in Chapter 2, separate accounts are a standard business practice for higher-level

I propose an alternative hypothesis. Rather than assuming that the traditional material exchange between husbands and wives is a necessary element of marital longevity, we might posit that the dissolution of separate spheres ought to give the marital bond a more creative and supportive foundation and encourage those same elements that traditional theories present as essential to marital longevity: intimacy, trust, and nurturance. When the underlying material exchange disappears, these elements no longer disguise in reverent tones the economic dominance of husbands over wives but come to have fuller meaning. In short, a dual-career marriage has the potential to be a more rather than a less durable relationship than the normative model.

Lest this proposition be interpreted as utopian, the framework of this question must be emphasized. First, dual-career couples are a special and contingent category of families. They are part of a social and economic elite within a capitalist society, and as such do not represent a modal form of marriage.

Second, the concern of dual-career couples for the marital bond—something that family traditionalists certainly would not have expected with women's employment—in some ways shares the contractual character of other kinds of careers. Couples, for example, deal with their individual and shared incomes in a way more remi-

---

corporate employees—for clothing, entertainment, travel, and so on—and it seems logical to extend this practice into the home. Second, such reactions reveal that money and financial decision making are touchy issues in most marriages. The departure from traditional practice that having separate accounts represents cannot help but highlight the question of money and equity in even the most liberal of households. Finally, such negative reactions demonstrate how deeply the normative model of marriage is ingrained in our consciousness. While not exactly knee-jerk in nature, the facile rejection of the dual-career/separate accounting/hired-labor model of marriage reveals how much we are all influenced by socialization and how difficult it is to question ideological (magical) assumptions and processes (misdirection).

niscent of a business partnership than of communal enterprises. Although they clearly do not calculate profit and loss, neither do they place as great an emphasis on "ours" as has been the case in traditional marriages. These couples also "subcontract" more and more family services in an effort to sustain the family unit and with it the careers they cherish. Thus, they convert more and more of their lives into commodities (goods and labor), while trying to protect the relationship they have with each other from being dissolved into a monetary exchange. The private purchase and consumption of those commodities allows a degree of intimacy and personal control, which is the saving grace offered by the first two careers. Thus, the dual-career family remains a "haven in a heartless world" (Lasch, 1977) only because it has been sufficiently successful in the heartless world to financially afford a haven.

# Appendix: Methodology

## SAMPLE DESIGN AND SELECTION

This study focused on married couples who had corporate careers in order to highlight the relationship between work and family for this interesting stratum of American society. Couples employed in corporate settings were chosen because they were expected to have limited discretion over their work schedules and to be more responsive to work assignments issued by superiors than would other categories of employees, such as professionals or academics, who have comprised the core respondents for much of the previous research on dual-career couples. In fact, a conscious decision was made to exclude academics from the sample. Academics traditionally have greater discretion over their schedules and are not normally expected to account for their whereabouts during time spent out of the office. I wanted to study couples in which both spouses were employed in rigid work settings so that type of employment would not determine who would be responsible for the domestic side of life. Further, because women are now entering corporations in positions traditionally held by men, I was interested in the corporate response, if any, to family life.

I also decided to interview both couples who had children and those who did not in order to gather information on their future plans for children—when they would have them and how they would manage childcare arrangements. I decided not to interview couples in which the wife had left the work force to have children and returned more than six months later or had quit her job altogether in order to have children.

Generating a sample of corporate dual-career couples proved a difficult undertaking. Cross-sectional surveys such as those of the Census Bureau identify two-earner families but do not specifically target couples with careers or two-career families with corporate employers. Surveys from other research organizations that might have unearthed a larger number of respondents generally did not provide a great deal of information on areas critical to my study (family and work histories, or financial accounting systems), nor did they include both spouses in their samples.

In the face of these limitations, I chose to generate my own sample. In order to find a sample of corporate dual-career couples, I initially attempted to gain access to these couples through the corporations themselves, believing that this would allow me to make systematic comparisons between corporations. The presidents or chief executive officers of three multinational corporations that I contacted were willing to cooperate. Memos were sent to middle managers and their superiors (in corporate headquarters) asking if their spouses also had careers in large corporations. Unfortunately, this approach produced only two or three names per corporate location. Had I pursued this strategy at a large number of sites, I might have identified enough couples in different locations to allow me to make the systematic corporate comparisons I had initially hoped for. But this approach had to be abandoned, as I did not have sufficient funding to travel to different parts of the country.

Because I was living in Chicago, a city in which numerous large corporations have headquarters, I decided to take a different tack, using a modified "snowball" sampling technique to locate appropriate couples. I began by calling all the acquaintances I or friends knew in the Chicago area who had corporate careers at the level of middle management or above. Each individual contacted was asked to provide the names of two-career corporate couples he or she knew. After identifying and interviewing an initial group of couples this way, I used them to expand the sample. If the spouses of the first dual-career couple I interviewed knew of only one couple, I asked the referral for one additional name. If the first couple gave me the names of two couples, I did not ask these additional couples for references. The process, designed to ensure that I was not just tapping one network in Chicago, netted a sample of forty-two individuals located in thirty-four different organizations in the Chicago metropolitan area.

No husband and wife within the same couple in this study worked for the same corporation, although several worked for competing firms. Only two individuals worked in nonprofit organizations: one, a medical doctor, worked for a health maintenance organization; another respondent was employed by a charity. As I discussed in Chapter 2, several other respondents left large corporations in order to start their own businesses. But in each of these cases, their spouses were employed in major Chicago corporations.

Although this was not a deliberate sampling strategy, all respondents were Caucasian.

## INTERVIEWING PROCEDURES AND FORMAT

Mentioning the name of the person who referred me, I contacted the recommended spouse. (Many times the reference person knew that both spouses were employed in corporate careers but only knew either the husband or the wife through business dealings.) I found that relying on referrals was extremely valuable, because people were willing to participate when they knew that a friend or acquaintance had already participated or recommended them. (Only one couple turned me down; both spouses were spending a lot of time traveling overseas.) I explained to the potential interviewee that I was interested in interviewing husbands and wives separately on the topic of family and work. In every case the person I initially called said that they would have to discuss participation in the study with their spouse and that they would call me back. No one agreed to participate without having discussed the matter with his or her spouse. Once the couple had discussed participation and consented to be interviewed, I arranged separate appointments with each spouse. The majority of the interviews took place in the respondent's office after 4:00 P.M. Individuals chose that location rather than their homes to allow more privacy and to reduce the chance of being disturbed by children or spouses. As evidence of the full work schedules these people have, almost all of them scheduled appointments a month in advance. A quarter of the respondents called the morning of the interview to reschedule as a result of last-minute business or travel plans or unanticipated meetings with superiors, usually rescheduling for the following month. In two cases, rescheduling of this kind occurred twice.

Interviews were planned around the work schedule of the other spouse. Husbands and wives were interviewed within ten weeks of each other. With the permission of the respondent, I taped each interview and then transcribed and coded it. Interviews lasted an average of two-and-a-half hours, and in several cases I followed up with a phone conversation. Respondents were guaranteed anonymity. For this reason names are changed in every quote, as are all comments that might identify specific corporations. The interviews were conducted in 1981 and 1982. Salary information pertained to calendar year 1981.

The interviews were conducted in a semi-structured format, based on a series of open-ended questions followed by intensive probes. All the respondents were asked an identical set of questions; the only exception to this was on the topic of maternity leaves for women. The following list of topics and sample questions represents the basic protocol I used in the interviews:

A. Background
   1. Career history
      a. List all the jobs and companies you have worked for since college.
   2. Marital history
      a. At what point in your career history did you get married?
      b. How many children do you have?
      c. What was the timing of your children's births?
   3. Relocation (moves)
      a. What was the impact on respondent, family, children?
      b. Tell me about your last move. Was this move different from other moves?

B. Impact of work on family
   1. Present job
      a. Tell me about your job. Take this past month: How long were you at home and away? Let's talk about yesterday: What hours did you work? When did you get home? Was the past week typical?
      b. Describe yesterday for me, from the time you got up until the time you went to bed.

c. When there are family problems—for example, sick children at home—do they affect your work habits?
d. Does your boss tell you when to travel, or do you plan your own travel schedule? Please explain. Do you take into account your family plans or social engagements? Do you check with your spouse first?

C. Impact of family on work
1. Cross-cutting responsibilities
   a. How much job-connected entertaining do you do?
   b. How much entertaining is related to your spouse's job?
   c. Is your family involved in your work in other ways?
2. Information sharing
   a. Do you talk about work with your spouse?
   b. What sorts of things do you talk about?
3. Spouse's influence on decision making at work
   a. What is your spouse's influence on hiring, firing, daily decisions?
   b. Do you have an influence on your spouse's decisions?
4. Spouse's influence on career
   a. Would you relocate with your spouse?
   b. Have you talked about relocating?
   c. From the corporate view, what happens to you if you refuse to relocate?
5. Perception of the corporation
   a. Is there an ideal "corporate spouse," from the point of view of your employer?
6. Critical incident
   a. Was there ever an incident where you felt your job affected your family negatively? And the converse?

   b. Was there ever an incident where you felt your job affected your family positively? And the converse?

D. Division of labor at home
   1. Household chores
      a. What arrangements do you have for getting household chores done?
      b. Who takes responsibility for what and for how long?
   2. Children and childcare (where applicable)
      a. What arrangements do you have for caring for the child(ren)? Why?
      b. Did you consider other alternative arrangements? Could you provide a history of your childcare arrangements (how you found each person, how you set costs)?
      c. Whose responsibility is it to supervise those arrangements? Why?
   3. Money matters
      a. How much do you earn? How about your spouse?
      b. Tell me how you use your paycheck. What sorts of things do you buy on your own and what things do you buy after discussion with your spouse?
      c. How do you handle the monthly bills in your family? What kind of accounting arrangement do you use?
      d. Have you always used this arrangement?
      e. What about business-related expenses?
      f. What about longer-term expenses or investments?

E. Children and careers
   1. Having children
      a. At what point will you/did you feel it possible to have children?

b. How did you arrive at that decision?
c. Did you feel pressured to have or not to have children? Why?
d. How did your employer respond? Why?

2. Children's perceptions
   a. How do your children feel about your work?
   b. Do they know what you do? How would they describe what you do?
3. Employer response
   a. How did your employer respond to your pregnancy?
   b. Were there maternity leave policies or daycare benefits at that time?
   c. What have others in the corporation done when they became pregnant?

F. Lifestyle
   1. Residence
      a. Are you satisfied living where you do?
      b. Would you rather continue living in the city/suburbs?
   2. Marriage and career
      a. How has your spouse been an asset (or a detriment) to your career?
      b. Is it important to be (and stay) married?
      c. Is it important to have children (or more children)?
   3. Adjustments
      a. What sort of adjustments do you think your family has made because of your present career?

G. Family background
   1. Did your mother work when you were growing up? Explain.
   2. Did your father work when you were growing up? Explain.

3. How many siblings do you have?
4. What was the class background of your parents?
5. What was your parents' marital status?
6. What were your parents' occupations?

I chose to interview husbands and wives separately and expected to find "two marriages—his and hers," as Bernard (1972) termed it. This was not the case at all. Instead, there was not only a similarity in responses, but husbands and wives were also likely to tell the same stories to illustrate a point. It is possible, given the time lag between interviewing husband and wife, that the first spouse discussed responses to questions with his or her mate. However, if this was the case, no individuals informed me that they had discussed my interview with their spouse. I found the respondents to be candid, open, and articulate in discussing their relationships. However, when I asked them how they felt about something, women were more likely to launch into lengthy discussions of their feelings, whereas men were more likely to keep their answers short or to tell me they never thought about how they felt. Other researchers have discussed men's lack of ability to express their feelings (Fasteau, 1975; Rubin, 1983); nevertheless, I wonder if my own concern as a woman with people's feelings about what they do may have made me somewhat more sensitive to the greater ability of women to express those feelings.

## DATA ANALYSIS AND PRESENTATION

Data were analyzed in two stages. In the first, the interview transcripts were read thoroughly (once they were transcribed from tape), and individual interviews were coded according to the major topic areas listed in the interview protocol. The topic areas were largely descriptive and attempted to encompass what were viewed at the outset as major dimensions of career and family and their interaction. However, as intended, coding and reading were iterative processes: more codes emerged and others changed as the interviews accumulated and my understanding increased. The area of family financial accounting systems is a case in point. I began the interviews with a set of questions about financial affairs that were part of my effort to go beyond the usual focus on household chores as an indicator of division of labor in the family. As I learned more about the material and symbolic importance of money, I began rereading earlier interviews with a new perspective and broadened my coding to take the new ideas into account. Once the interviews were completed, I had rather substantially amended the coding scheme. Each interview was then summarized along topical lines.

The second stage of data analysis involved the coding of basic demographic, marital, occupational, educational, and income information for each respondent. These data were then transferred to a computer file for subsequent calculation of frequencies and simple cross tabulations.

In presenting the findings from this research, I had two objectives in mind: First, I wanted to avoid the appearance of homogeneity in these couples' attitudes and behaviors. Thus, where and when possible, I have presented assenting and dissenting views on particular topics and at the same time given an indication of the relative distribution of each. I did this in recognition of the relatively small sample size and in an effort to demonstrate the variability of response within a limited sample.

Second, I devoted considerable space to the couples' own words. I wanted to capture their situation as they told it so that the reader would have a sense of how these couples perceived their work and family lives. These frequent and occasionally lengthy excerpts from the interviews do not, of course, substitute for my own analysis. However, it is testimony to the value of the qualitative methodology that their words forced me to continuously question and revise my own preconceived ideas.

# References


Angrist, Shirley S., Judith R. Lave, and Richard Mickelsen

1976 "How Working Mothers Manage: Socioeconomic Differences in Work, Childcare, and Household Tasks." *Social Science Quarterly* 56 (March): 631–637.

Bailyn, Lotte

1970 "Career and Family Orientation of Husbands and Wives in Relation to Marital Happiness." *Human Relations* 22:97–113.

Bart, Pauline

1972 "Depression in Middle-Aged Women." In *Women in Sexist Society: Studies in Power and Powerlessness,* ed. Vivian Gornick and Barbara K. Moran, 162–186. New York: Basic Books.

1975 "The Loneliness of the Long-Distance Mother." In *Women: A Feminist Perspective,* ed. Jo Freeman, 156–170. Palo Alto, Calif.: Mayfield.

Bebbington, A. C.

1973 "The Function of Stress in the Establishment of the Dual-Career Family." *Journal of Marriage and the Family* 35, no. 3 (August): 530–537.

Berger, Brigitte, and Peter Berger

1983 *War over the Family: Capturing the Middle Ground.* New York: Anchor.

Berk, Richard, and Sarah F. Berk

1979 *Labor and Leisure at Home: Content and Organization of the Household Day*. Beverly Hills, Calif.: Sage.

Bernard, Jessie
1972 *The Future of Marriage.* New York: Bantam Books.

Berstein, Leonard
1983 "Heckler Says Child Care Good Business." *Hartford Courant,* 22 June, 6.

Bird, Caroline
1979 *The Two-Paycheck Marriage.* New York: Pocket Books.

Blood, Robert O., and Donald M. Wolfe
1960 *Husbands and Wives.* New York: Free Press.

Blumberg, Rae Lasser
1977 "Women and Work Around the World." In *Beyond Sex Roles,* ed. Alice G. Sargent, 412–433. St. Paul, Minn.: West.

Bryson, Rebecca, Jeff B. Bryson, and Marilyn F. Johnson
1978 "Family Size, Satisfaction, and Productivity in Dual-Career Couples." *Psychology of Women Quarterly* 3:167–177.

*Business Week*
1978 "The Upward Mobility Two Incomes Can Buy." 20 February, 80–86.
1981 "America's New Immobile Society." 27 July, 58–62.

*Chicago Tribune*
1980 "Jobs Keep Couples Cities Apart," by Martha Groves. 20 July, 1, 3 (Business section).
1981a "Love and Work," by Linda Wolfe. 8 March, 1–3 (Lifestyle section).
1981b "Stress in Two-Career Families Puts Pressure on Employers, Too," by Elaine Markoutas. 26 July, 1.
1982 "Couples' Dual Goals Pose Problems of Priorities," by Janet Key. 12 October, H1.

Chodorow, Nancy
1978 *The Reproduction of Mothering: Psychoanalysis and the Sociology of Gender.* Berkeley and Los Angeles: University of California Press.

Daniels, Pamela, and Kathy Weingarten
1982 *Sooner or Later: The Timing of Parenthood in Adult Life.* New York: W. W. Norton.

Dinnerstein, Dorothy
1976 *The Mermaid and the Minotaur: Sexual Arrangements and Human Malaise.* New York: Harper & Row.

Dizard, Jan
1968 *Social Change in the Family.* Chicago: University of Chicago Press.

Edwards, Richard C.
1979 *Contested Terrain: The Transformation of the Workplace in the Twentieth Century.* New York: Basic Books.

Emlen, Arthur C., Betty A. Donoghue, and Quentin D. Clarkson
1974 *The Stability of the Family Daycare Arrangement: A Longitudinal Study.* Corvallis, Ore.: A Continuing Education Publication.

Fasteau, Marc F.
1975 *The Male Machine.* New York: Delta.

Firestone, Shulamith
1970 *The Dialectic of Sex: The Case for Feminist Revolution.* New York: Morrow.

Floge, Liliane
1985 "The Dynamics of Child-Care Use and Some Implications for Women's Employment." *Journal of Marriage and the Family* 47, no. 1 (February): 143–154.

Fraiberg, Selma
1977 *Every Child's Birthright.* New York: Basic Books.

Friedan, Betty
1963 *The Feminine Mystique.* New York: Dell.
1981 *The Second Stage.* New York: Simon & Schuster.

Fusfeld, Daniel
1973 *The Basic Economics of the Urban Racial Crisis.* New York: Holt, Rinehart & Winston.

Garland, T. Neal
1972 "The Better Half: The Male in the Dual-Career Professional Family." In *Toward a Sociology of Women,* ed. Constantina Safilios-Rothschild, 199–216. Lexington, Mass.: Xerox College Publishing.

Gerstel, Naomi, and Harriet Gross
1984 *Commuter Marriage.* New York: Guilford Press.

Gilbert, Lucia Albino
1985 *Men in Dual-Career Families: Current Realities and Future Prospects.* Hillsdale, N.J.: Lawrence Erlbaum Associates.

Greiff, Barrie S., and Preston K. Munter
1979 *Tradeoffs: Executive, Family, and Organizational Life.* New York: Simon & Schuster.

Hall, Francine S., and Douglas T. Hall
1979 *The Two-Career Couple.* Reading, Mass.: Addison-Wesley.

Hartmann, Heidi
1981a "The Unhappy Marriage of Marxism and Feminism: Toward a More Progressive Union." In *Women and Revolution,* ed. Lydia Sargent, 1–41. Boston: South End Press.
1981b "The Family as the Locus of Gender, Class, and Political Struggle: The Example of Housework." *Signs* 6:366–394.

Helsing, Knud J., Moyses Szklo, and George W. Comstock
1981 "Factors Associated with Mortality after Widowhood." *American Journal of Public Health* 71: 802–809.

Hochschild, Arlie
1971 "Inside the Clockwork of Male Careers." In *Women and the Power to Change,* ed. Florence Howe, 47–80. New York: McGraw-Hill.
1975 "Sociology of Feeling and Emotion: Selected Possibilities." In *Another Voice: Feminist Perspectives on Social Life and Social Science,* ed. Marcia

Millman and Rosabeth Kanter, 280–307. New York: Doubleday.

Hoffman, Lois W., and Ivan F. Nye
1974 *Working Mothers.* San Francisco, Calif.: Jossey-Bass.

Holmstrom, Lynda Lytle
1973 *The Two-Career Family.* Cambridge, Mass.: Schenkman.

Horner, Matina S.
1969 "Fail: Bright Women." *Psychology Today,* November, 36–38.
1972 "Toward an Understanding of Achievement-Related Conflicts in Women." *Journal of Social Issues* 28:157–175.

Houseknecht, Sharon K., and Anne S. Macke
1981 "Combining Marriage and Career: The Marital Adjustment of Professional Women." *Journal of Marriage and the Family* 43, no. 3 (August): 651–661.

Hunt, Janet G., and Larry L. Hunt
1977 "Dilemmas and Contradictions of Status: The Case of the Dual-Career Family." *Social Problems* 24:407–416.

Jones, Beverly
1970 "The Dynamics of Marriage and Motherhood." In *Sisterhood Is Powerful,* ed. Robin Morgan, 46–61. New York: Vintage Books.

Kanter, Rosabeth M.
1976 "The Impact of Hierarchical Structures on the Work Behavior of Men and Women." *Social Problems* 23 (April): 415–430.
1977 *Men and Women of the Corporation.* New York: Basic Books.

Keohane, Nannerl O., Michelle Z. Rosaldo, and Barbara C. Gelpi, eds.
1982 *Feminist Theory: A Critique of Ideology.* Chicago: University of Chicago Press.

Lasch, Christopher
1977 *Haven in a Heartless World: The Family Besieged.* New York: Basic Books.

Lein, Laura
1979 "Parental Evaluation of Childcare Alternatives." *Urban and Social Change Review* 12:11–16.

MacKinnon, Catherine
1981 "Feminism, Marxism, Method, and the State: An Agenda for Theory." In *Feminist Theory: A Critique of Ideology,* ed. Nannerl O. Keohane, Michelle Z. Rosaldo, and Barbara C. Gelpi, 1–30. Chicago: University of Chicago Press.

Margolis, Diane Rothbard
1979 *The Managers: Corporate Life in America.* New York: William Morrow.

Martin, Thomas W., Kenneth J. Berry, and R. Brooke Jacobsen
1975 "The Impact of Dual-Career Marriages on Female Professional Careers: An Empirical Test of a Parsonian Hypothesis." *Journal of Marriage and the Family* 37, no. 4 (November): 734–742.

McDonald, Gerald
1980 "Family Power: The Assessment of a Decade of Theory and Research, 1970–1979." *Journal of Marriage and the Family* 42, no. 4 (November): 841–854.

Meissner, Martin, Elizabeth W. Humphreys, Scott M. Meis, and William J. Scheu
1975 "No Exit for Wives: Equal Division of Labor and the Cumulation of Household Demands." *Canadian Review of Sociology and Anthropology* 12:424–439.

Miller, S. M.
1972 "The Making of a Confused Middle-Aged Husband." In *Toward a Sociology of Women,* ed. Constantina Safilios-Rothschild, 245–254. Lexington, Mass.: Xerox College Publishing.

Mills, C. Wright
1959 *The Sociological Imagination.* New York: Oxford University Press.

Mitchell, Juliet
1966 "Women: The Longest Revolution." *New Left Review* 40 (November/December): 11–37.

Model, Suzanne
1982 "Housework by Husbands: Determinants and Implications." In *Two Paychecks: Life in Dual-Earner Families,* ed. Joan Aldous, 193–206. Beverly Hills, Calif.: Sage.

*Newsweek*
1981a "The Baby Boomers Come of Age." 30 March, 34–37.
1981b "Women and the Executive Suite." 14 September, 65–68.

*New York Times*
1980a "Finding the Right Career-Family Mix," by Judy Klemesrud. 20 July, 36.
1980b "Many Young Women Now Say They'd Pick Family Over Career," by Dena Kleiman. 28 December, 1, 15.
1983a "Rise in Childbearing Found Among Women in 30s," by Robert Pear. 10 June, 12.
1983b "What's New with Dual-Career Couples," by Philip Shenon. 6 March, F29.

*New York Times Magazine*
1981 "The Perils of a Two-Income Family," by Didi Moore. 27 September, 91–96.
1982 "Careers and the Lure of Motherhood," by Anita Shreve. 21 November, 38–56.

Nye, Ivan F., and Lois W. Hoffman, eds.
1963 *The Employed Mother in America.* Chicago: Rand McNally.

Oppenheimer, Valerie K.
1976 *The Female Labor Force in the United States: Demographic and Economic Factors Governing Its Growth and Changing Composition.* Population

Monograph Series, no. 5. Westport, Conn.: Greenwood.

Papanek, Hanna
1975 "Men, Women, and Work: Reflections on the Two-Person Career." *American Journal of Sociology* 78:852–872.

Parsons, Talcott, and Robert F. Bales
1955 *Family, Socialization, and Interaction Process.* Glencoe, Ill.: Free Press.

Perrucci, Carolyn C., Harry R. Potter, and Deborah L. Rhoads
1978 "Determinants of Male Family-Role Performance." *Psychology of Women Quarterly* 3:153–166.

Pleck, Joseph H.
1977 "The Work-Family Role System." *Social Problems* 24:417–427.

Poloma, Margaret M., and T. Neal Garland
1971 "The Married Professional Woman: A Study in the Tolerance of Domestication." *Journal of Marriage and the Family* 33, no. 3 (August): 531–540.

Praeger, Susan Westerberg
1982 "Shifting Perspectives on Marital Property Law." In *Rethinking the Family: Some Feminist Questions,* ed. Barrie Thorne, 111–130. New York: Longman.

Rapoport, Rhona, and Robert N. Rapoport
1971 *Dual-Career Families.* Harmondsworth, England: Penguin Books.
1976 *Dual-Career Families Re-Examined: New Integrations of Work and Family.* New York: Harper & Row.

Robinson, John N.
1980 "Household Technology and Household Work." In *Women and Household Labor,* ed. Sarah F. Berk, 53–63. Beverly Hills, Calif.: Sage.

Robinson, J., T. Juster, and F. Stafford
1976 *Americans' Use of Time.* Ann Arbor, Mich.: Institute for Social Research.

Rossi, Alice
1964 "Equity Between the Sexes: An Immodest Proposal." *Daedalus* 93:607–652.
1968 "Transition to Parenthood." *Journal of Marriage and the Family* 30, no. 1 (February): 26–39.

Rubin, Lillian
1976 *Worlds of Pain: Life in the Working-Class Family.* New York: Basic Books.
1979 *Women of a Certain Age: The Midlife Search for Self.* New York: Harper & Row.
1983 *Intimate Strangers: Men and Women Together.* New York: Harper & Row.

Safilios-Rothschild, Constantina
1970a "The Study of Family Power Structure: A Review of 1960–1969." *Journal of Marriage and the Family* 32, no. 4 (November): 539–551.
1970b "The Influence of the Wife's Degree of Work Commitment upon Some Aspects of Family Organization and Dynamics." *Journal of Marriage and the Family* 32, no. 4 (November): 681–691.

Schnaiberg, Allan
1980 *The Environment: From Surplus to Scarcity.* New York: Oxford University Press.

Seidenberg, Robert
1975 *Corporate Wives—Corporate Casualties.* New York: American Management Association.

Sheehy, Gail
1977 *Passages: Predictable Crises of Adult Life.* New York: Bantam Books.

Smith, Dorothy
1975–1976 "Women, the Family, and Corporate Capitalism." *Berkeley Journal of Sociology* 20:55–90.

Spector, Malcolm, and John I. Kitsuse
1977 *Constructing Social Problems.* Menlo Park, Calif.: Benjamin Cummings.

Stack, Carol B.
1975 *All Our Kin: Strategies for Survival in a Black Community.* New York: Harper & Row.

Steinberg, L., and C. Green
1979 "What Parents Seek in Daycare." *Human Ecology Forum* 10(Fall): 13–14, 38–40.

Talmon, Yonina
1972 *Family and Community in the Kibbutz.* Cambridge, Mass.: Harvard University Press.

*Time*
1978a "America's New Elite." 21 August.
1978b "Marriage of the Minds." 6 March.
1985 "The Perils of Dual Careers." 13 May.

Thorne, Barrie
1982 "Feminist Rethinking of the Family: An Overview." In *Rethinking the Family,* ed. Barrie Thorne, 1–24. New York: Longman.

Thurow, Lester
1980 *The Zero-Sum Society: Distribution and the Possibilities for Economic Change.* New York: Basic Books.

U.S. Bureau of the Census
1980 Population Profile of the U.S. *Current Population Reports,* series P-20, no. 363. Washington, D.C.: U.S. Government Printing Office.
1981 Earnings Profile of U.S. Families. *Current Population Reports,* series CP-20. Washington, D.C.: U.S. Government Printing Office.
1983 Fertility of American Women: June 1982 (Advanced Report). *Current Population Reports,* series P-20, no. 379. Washington, D.C.: U.S. Government Printing Office.
1984 Fertility of American Women: June 1982. *Current Population Reports,* series P-20, no. 387. Washington, D.C.: U.S. Government Printing Office.

Vandervelde, Maryanne
1979 *The Changing Life of the Corporate Wife.* New York: Warner Books.

Veevers, Jean E.
1973 "Voluntary Childless Wives." *Sociology and Social Research* 57:356–366.

*Wall Street Journal*

1980a "Dual Incomes Will Lift More Families to Middle-Class Affluence in the Decade." 27 June, 27.

1980b "Inflation Toll Is Higher on One-Paycheck Families." 2 September, 3.

Walker, Kathryn E.

1970 "Time Spent by Husbands in Household Work." *Family Economics Review* 4, no. 2 (June): 8–11.

Weingarten, Kathy

1978 "The Employment Pattern of Professional Couples and Their Distribution of Involvement in the Family." *Psychology of Women Quarterly* 3:43–53.

Whyte, William H., Jr.

1951 "The Wives of Management." *Fortune,* October, 86–88, 204–213; November, 109–111, 150–158.

1952 "The Wife Problem." *Life,* January, 32–48.

1956 *The Organization Man.* New York: Simon & Schuster.

Wilensky, Harold

1960 "Work, Careers, and Social Integration." *International Social Science Journal* 12 (Fall): 543–560.

1961 "Orderly Careers and Social Participation: The Impact of Work History on Social Integration in the Middle Mass." *American Sociological Review* 26 (August): 521–539.

Yogev, Sara

1981 "Do Professional Women Have Egalitarian Marital Relationships?" *Journal of Marriage and the Family* 43, no. 4 (November): 865–871.

Young, Michael, and Peter Willmott

1973 *The Symmetrical Family.* New York: Pantheon.

Zaretsky, Eli

1982 "The Place of the Family in the Origins of the Welfare State." In *Rethinking the Family: Some Feminist Questions,* ed. Barrie Thorne, 188–224. New York: Longman.

# Index

| | |
|---|---|
| Compositor: | Huron Valley Graphics |
| Printer: | Vail-Ballou Press |
| Binder: | Vail-Ballou Press |
| Text: | 11/13 Baskerville |
| Display: | Baskerville |